Hell
God's Prison

By Gary P. Miller

Published by Grace Harbor Church
www.grace-harbor-church.org

ISBN: 978-1-60208-341-7

Dedicated to those who stand in the light of God's truth.

The light of the scriptures will reveal what the unrighteous will find behind death's darkened door,
HELL.

Psa. 119:130
The entrance of thy words giveth light; it giveth understanding unto the simple.

INTRODUCTION

The flames of Hell have been burning for over 6,000 thousand years. Hell and its torments have influenced man's culture, religion, and society since man was created. All men know that Hell is downward.

The purpose of this book is to help believers have a sound Biblical understanding of the doctrine of Hell. The scriptures teach a lot about Hell, its purpose, the change it experienced because of Calvary, and it's future destination. Understanding the past, present, and future of Hell should encourage saints in their witness of God's great salvation.

2 Cor. 5:11a Knowing therefore the terror of the Lord, we persuade men

We will see how God meets both the righteous and unrighteous at death and learn about the pathway that the soul travels to reach Hell. The structure and interior of Hell will be revealed as the scriptures lead us down toward the great furnace that heats both Hell and the earth itself. Once inside Hell, we will learn what happens to the souls, what they do, and the social order that exists.

We will go into the courtroom of God to understand Satan's interest in Hell, and how he tried to use it to thwart God's promise in Gen. 3:15. We will witness what took place on the cross of Calvary and why Christ went to Hell after He gave up the ghost. This book will reveal what Christ did in Hell and why the gates of Hell could not prevail against Him.

6

We will see Hell fulfill its purpose, emptied, and finally disposed of. The distinctions between Hell and the Lake of Fire will be shown. God's justice will be discussed as it is executed perfectly, for all of eternity, on the unrighteous.

So let us turn to the scriptures and learn from God what He has written about Hell.

Table of Contents

8

Preface

Before we begin our study about Hell, we first want to look at how God created man.

Gen. 2:7 And the LORD God formed man of the dust of the ground, and breathed into his nostrils the breath of life; and man became a living soul.

Man's physical body is "formed" from the dust of the earth and is indwelt by a soul and spirit. All men are created with a body of flesh, a soul, and a spirit.

The body of flesh does not live forever; it dies. Physical death occurs when man's spirit leaves his body.

Jam. 2:26a For as the body without the spirit is dead,

At death the body returns to the dust of the earth.

Ecc. 3:20 All go unto one place; all are of the dust, and all turn to dust again.

There is no question as to where the body goes when it dies. What we want to talk about in this book is where the spirit and soul go at death.

The spirit and soul are eternal and will live forever after the physical body dies.

Heb. 9:27 And as it is appointed unto men once to die, but after this the judgment:

This verse teaches that all men die and that no man can escape their appointment with death. This verse goes on to say that all men will face judgment after death; there will be a judgment day.

Men's souls are not judged immediately upon death, the judgment of Heb. 9:27 speaks about a judgment to come, a future judgment. Because this judgment is future, God prepared a place for the souls of men to go to and await judgment. The Bible calls this place Hell.[1]

---

[1] We shall see that prior to Calvary all souls went to Hell, both the righteous and the unrighteous. After Calvary, the lost continue to go to Hell, but the saved go to be with the Lord in Heaven.

CHAPTER 1

HELL

Hell is not a figment of imagination or a fable. It is a real place with a physical location, structure, design, and purpose. Let us first look at how the Bible describes Hell as a real place.

God created a place that He called "Hell".

- Hell is a literal, physical place -

Psa. 55:18a Let death seize upon them, and let them go down quick into hell:

2 Pet. 2:4a For if God spared not the angels that sinned, but cast them down to hell,

The above verses show Hell to be a real place.

Job 11:8 It is as high as heaven; what canst thou do? deeper than hell; what canst thou know?

This verse speaks of both Heaven and Hell; both are real places.

The Lord Jesus Christ speaks about Hell as being a real place in the following verses.

Mat. 11:23a And thou, Capernaum, which art exalted unto heaven, shalt be brought down to hell:

Mat. 5:29 And if thy right eye offend thee, pluck it out, and cast it from thee: for it is profitable for thee that one of thy members should perish, and not that thy whole body should be cast into hell.

Mark9:45 And if thy foot offend thee, cut it off: it is better for thee to enter halt into life, than having two feet to be cast into hell, into the fire that never shall be quenched:

"The pit" is another name for Hell in the scriptures.

Isa. 14:15 Yet thou shalt be brought down to hell, to the sides of the pit.

Eze. 31:16a I made the nations to shake at the sound of his fall, when I cast him down to hell with them that descend into the pit:

It is clear from the above verses that "hell" and "the pit" are the same place. "Hell" and "the pit" are many times used interchangeably in scripture and they describe a real place.

We will now look at the characteristics of Hell, its location, appearance, and interior, prior to the change it experienced after Calvary.

- Hell's Location -

When people, saints and heathen alike, think about the location of Hell they invariably point downward. They are correct; it is down.

Isa. 14:15 Yet thou shalt be brought down to hell, to the sides of the pit.

Psa. 55:15a Let death seize upon them, and let them go down quick into hell:

Eze. 31:17a They also went down into hell with him unto them that be slain with the sword;

In these three verses Hell is "down", "down", "down" in the earth. In fact, in Amos 9:2 we read that one could "dig" and reach Hell.

Amo. 9:2 Though they dig into hell, thence shall mine hand take them; though they climb up to heaven, thence will I bring them down:

When Korah and his followers resisted the authority of Moses, the Lord opened the earth creating a shaft that led straight down to Hell.

Num. 16:31-33 And it came to pass, as he had made an end of speaking all these words, that the ground clave asunder that was under them:
And the earth opened her mouth, and swallowed them up, and their houses, and all the men that appertained unto Korah, and all their goods.
They, and all that appertained to them, went down alive into the pit, and the earth closed upon them: and they perished from among the congregation.

This was a frightening sight for Israel to behold, seeing the bodies fall straight into "the pit" or Hell. If they had looked down into the opening of the earth, they would have been looking down into the mouth of Hell.

Hell is not only down in the earth; it is located in the lowest parts of the earth.

Eze. 26:20a When I shall bring thee down with them that descend into the pit, with the people of old time, and shall set thee in the low parts of the earth,

Eze. 32:24 There is Elam and all her multitude round about her grave, all of them slain, fallen by the sword, which are gone down uncircumcised into the nether parts of the earth, which caused their terror in the land of the living; yet have they borne their shame with them that go down to the pit.

The "nether" or "low" parts of the earth are where Hell is found. It is under the oceans and mountains, in the lowest parts of the earth.

Much can be learned about the location of Hell from Jonah. When the whale swallowed Jonah, he died and went to Hell. His physical body remained three days in the belly of the whale, but his soul went to Hell.

Jon. 2:2 And said, I cried by reason of mine affliction unto the LORD, and he heard me; out of the belly of hell cried I, and thou heardest my voice.

Jonah cried out of the "belly of hell", Hell here is not the belly of the whale, but Hell itself.

Jonah described what he saw on his journey down to Hell.

Jon. 2:6 I went down to the bottoms of the mountains; the earth with her bars was about me for ever: yet

hast thou brought up my life from corruption, O LORD my God.

As he came closer to Hell he knew that he was at the very "bottoms of the mountains". The mountains stretch upward on all sides leaving him feeling surrounded, enclosed, and trapped. To be under all the mountains one would have to be in the very center of the earth. The center of the earth would also be the "low parts", "nether" parts of the earth. Hell is located in the very center of the earth.

Cross section of the earth

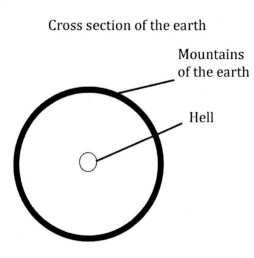

Mountains
of the earth

Hell

- The Exterior of Hell -

The scriptures provide a vivid picture of how Hell is constructed and what it looks like.

Continuing on in Jonah, he described another feature of Hell.

Jon. 2:6 I went down to the bottoms of the mountains; the earth with her bars was about me for ever: yet hast thou brought up my life from corruption, O LORD my God.

Jonah described seeing "bars". These bars encompassed him, they were "forever about" him. Everywhere he looked he saw bars. Jonah is telling us that Hell is surrounded by bars.

Job also speaks about bars surrounding Hell.

Job 17:16 They shall go down to the bars of the pit, when our rest together is in the dust.

Both Jonah and Job tell us that there are "bars" that surround Hell. Why are there bars around Hell?

Bars are used to keep people from leaving places. Imagine a prison, the windows and doors are made of bars. In fact, prisons are surrounded by bars or fences. The grounds leading into the prison are often lined with rows upon rows of fences, all with the purpose of keeping people inside. The same is true of Hell; bars surround it, and stretch in every direction, as far as Jonah could see. The bars of Hell are there to do what bars are intended to do, to confine the occupants and to keep them from escaping.

Hell's location in the center of the earth, at the bottom of the mountains, surrounded by bars all contribute to its purpose. Hell is designed to prohibit escape for those awaiting God's judgment.

Hell is built like a prison. Consequently, Hell is a prison.

If one were to visit a prison, one would be looking at a structure patterned after Hell. Prisons are many times put in remote areas. Fences, barbed wire, and bars surround prisons. As one enters a prison the feeling of being confined by bars is very sobering as one is marched through the intricate metal jungle. The bars tower over you as they stretch in every direction, destroying any possible hope of escape. This is how God designed Hell. It is a prison built to prevent the escape of those who are incarcerated there.

In fact, Hell is called a prison in the scriptures.

Isa. 24:22 And they shall be gathered together, as prisoners are gathered in the pit, and shall be shut up in the prison, and after many days shall they be visited.

In this verse "the pit" is Hell and it is called a "prison".

Isaiah mentions this "prison" again a few chapters later.

Isa. 42:7 To open the blind eyes, to bring out the prisoners from the prison, and them that sit in darkness out of the prison house.

Isaiah 42:7 is prophecy concerning Christ. One of His activities while He was in Hell was to lead the "prisoners" "out of the prison house". The "prison house" in this verse is Hell. We will explain His visit to this "prison" in chapter 10.

Psalms 142:7 is a prayer of Jesus Christ as He called upon God the Father from Hell.[2]

Psa. 142:7 Bring my soul out of prison, that I may praise thy name: the righteous shall compass me about; for thou shalt deal bountifully with me.

Jesus Christ called Hell, "prison".

As one would expect, a prison houses prisoners. God calls those who are in Hell, "prisoners" as seen in Isa. 24:22 & 42:7 - "as prisoners are gathered in the pit", "to bring out the prisoners from the prison,".

All prisons have a gate to allow entry; the same is true of Hell. Hell has a main gate or entrance that scripture refers to as a "mouth".

Psa. 69:15 Let not the waterflood overflow me, neither let the deep swallow me up, and let not the pit shut her mouth upon me.

Isa. 4:14 Therefore hell hath enlarged herself, and opened her mouth without measure: and their glory, and their multitude, and their pomp, and he that rejoiceth, shall descend into it.

This "mouth" of Hell is a gate, which opens to receive the "prisoners" as they enter and closes behind them. It can be "opened" and "shut".

When the "mouth" is open to receive prisoners, the interior of Hell is visible and accessible.

---

[2] Chapter 8 will discuss Jesus Christ in Hell.

- The Interior of Hell -

We learn about the interior of Hell from the Lord Jesus Christ in His account of the rich man and Lazarus as found in Luke.

Luk. 16:22-26 And it came to pass, that the beggar died, and was carried by the angels into Abraham's bosom: the rich man also died, and was buried;
And in hell he lift up his eyes, being in torments, and seeth Abraham afar off, and Lazarus in his bosom.
And he cried and said, Father Abraham, have mercy on me, and send Lazarus, that he may dip the tip of his finger in water, and cool my tongue; for I am tormented in this flame.
But Abraham said, Son, remember that thou in thy lifetime receivedst thy good things, and likewise Lazarus evil things: but now he is comforted, and thou art tormented.
And beside all this, between us and you there is a great gulf fixed: so that they which would pass from hence to you cannot; neither can they pass to us, that would come from thence.

We see from these verses that Hell consists of two different compartments. There is one side that the rich man finds himself in and another side where Lazarus is found. These are two distinct and separate areas in Hell. The side that Lazarus is on is called "Abraham's bosom". The other side that the rich man is in is a place of torments. There is a gulf that separates these two compartments. This divide is great and cannot be crossed.

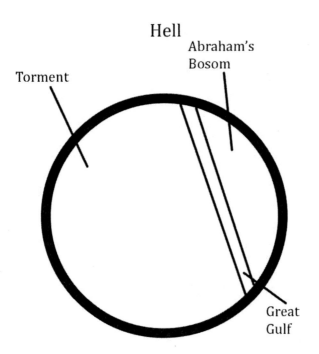

Lazarus was in a place of comfort, Abraham's bosom. God designed it as a place of rest and blessing for the righteous.

Across the gulf, on the other side of Hell, is found the place of torment. The torment side contains none of the comforts of Abraham's bosom. There is not even a drop of water to be found. The unrighteous on this side live in "torments". The grief and hopelessness felt by those on this side of Hell is surely as great as the gulf before them.

Let's look at the torment side of Hell. The torments found here are never ending and constantly afflict those within with the most excruciating prods of pain and suffering.

It is hot; the heat and flames cause anguish and suffering for those found there.

Luk. 16:24 And he cried and said, Father Abraham, have mercy on me, and send Lazarus, that he may dip the tip of his finger in water, and cool my tongue; for I am tormented in this flame.

The unrighteous are "tormented in this flame". They are actually not just hot, but in the flame.

Jesus Christ referred to the flames of "hell fire" that are found in Hell. These flames are real and afflict those who are in them.

Mat. 18:9 And if thine eye offend thee, pluck it out, and cast it from thee: it is better for thee to enter into life with one eye, rather than having two eyes to be cast into hell fire.

This fire and its flames fill the torment side of Hell. There is no place that the fires of Hell have not traveled nor left untouched. They completely engulf this side, from the floor to the ceiling; there is no escaping them. The roaring sounds of the fires are mingled with the screams of those who are scorched within.

The torment side of Hell has a number of levels.

Deu. 32:22 For a fire is kindled in mine anger, and shall burn unto the lowest hell, and shall consume the earth with her increase, and set on fire the foundations of the mountains.

22

Psa. 88:6 Thou hast laid me in the lowest pit, in darkness, in the deeps.

After entering the "mouth" of Hell, the prisoners will find a long descending path that goes lower and lower into depths of torment. When the scriptures say "lowest hell" we learn that there are levels in Hell, some parts being lower than others.

As the unrighteous travel down the path into Hell, they will notice that there are rooms along the sides of the passageway.

Isa.14:15 Yet thou shalt be brought down to hell, to the sides of the pit.

Eze. 32:23a Whose graves are set in the sides of the pit,

These verses tell us that Hell has "sides" in it. Much like a prison that we are familiar with, Hell has cells, rooms, cavities, or chambers[3] along its corridors. These chambers are along the sides of the pit and are found along the different levels of Hell.

Isaiah describes Hell as containing "stones".

Isa. 14:19b that go down to the stones of the pit;

Stone is hard, unforgiving, and uncomfortable. When heated by flames it is hot and burning. Every surface one

---

[3]They are also called "chambers of death" in Proverbs.
Prov. 7:27 Her house is the way to hell, going down to the chambers of death.

touches is scorching and painful. There is no rest as one is constantly moving trying to avoid the searing heat.

There is darkness in Hell.

Psa. 88:6 Thou hast laid me in the lowest pit, in darkness, in the deeps.

Darkness is in the lowest areas of Hell.

There is an area in Hell where angels are being held prisoner. God imprisoned angels here and is holding them until He judges them for their sins. Peter tells us they are imprisoned and held fast by "chains of darkness".

2 Pet. 2:4 For if God spared not the angels that sinned, but cast them down to hell, and delivered them into chains of darkness, to be reserved unto judgment;

If one were to travel all the way down the descending pathway of Hell they would arrive at the center of Hell. The bottomless pit is located here.

Rev. 9:1-2 And the fifth angel sounded, and I saw a star fall from heaven unto the earth: and to him was given the key of the bottomless pit.
And he opened the bottomless pit; and there arose a smoke out of the pit, as the smoke of a great furnace; and the sun and the air were darkened by reason of the smoke of the pit.

But what does it mean to be bottomless? How can a pit be bottomless? If the bottomless pit were at the very center of the earth, it would mean that one could no more go downward. If one were to travel in any direction from the very center of the earth one would be going upward, toward the surface. This "bottomless pit" is at the very bottom of the earth, the center; there is no further down to go, thus it is bottomless. The bottomless pit is in Hell, and is a part of Hell.

The bottomless pit is a "great furnace" and exceedingly hot.[4] Hell is heated from this place to such an extent that the flames torment the rich man in an upper level of Hell. The closer one gets to the bottomless pit, the greater the intensity of the heat.

Hell can be moved and stirred.

Isa. 14:9 Hell from beneath is moved for thee to meet thee at thy coming: it stirreth up the dead for thee, even all the chief ones of the earth; it hath raised up from their thrones all the kings of the nations.

Much like an earthquake, Hell can be moved and stirred, causing the occupants to be shaken out of their holes, cells, the sides of the pit.

The Bible has shown that Hell is constructed and designed as a prison. It is located in the center of the

---

[4] Man knows that the center of the earth is exceedingly hot, that the core has temperatures that reach into the thousands of degrees. This heat from the earth's core is seen in the violent volcanic activity around the globe. The scriptures state that there is a furnace in the bottomless pit. It is this furnace that is causing the heat generated in the core of the earth. Scientist would be wise to believe the Bible.
Job 28:5 As for the earth, out of it cometh bread: and under it is turned up as it were fire.

earth. It was divided into two parts, Abraham's bosom and a side of torment. Abraham's bosom was a place of comfort and rest. The torment side is a place of intense torments of fire and flames, consisting of stones and has levels descending downward. Along the descending corridor there are cells, rooms, or chambers on the sides of Hell. At the center of Hell is the bottomless pit.

The scriptures also tell us that Hell has been enlarged.

Isa. 4:14 Therefore hell hath enlarged herself, and opened her mouth without measure: and their glory, and their multitude, and their pomp, and he that rejoiceth, shall descend into it.

The enlargement of Hell was made necessary due to the increase in the amount of souls entering.

Mat. 7:13 Enter ye in at the strait gate: for wide is the gate, and broad is the way, that leadeth to destruction, and many there be which go in thereat:

As more and more beings were confined in Hell, it had to grow to meet the demand. Just as a prison that starts out small, but needs to be expanded as more and more criminals are incarcerated there, so it was with Hell. God increased the size of Hell to provide for all the beings imprisoned there. God's enlargement of Hell is His response to those who stand in opposition to Him and die in rebellion and unbelief.

Hell was specifically designed and built to hold the creatures that where placed inside of it. Hell was built to be a prison, thus Hell is God's prison.

CHAPTER 2

THE INHABITANTS OF HELL

God built His prison to house inmates. We will now look at the creatures that inhabit Hell.

The first group we will look at is angels.

2 Pet. 2:4 For if God spared not the angels that sinned, but cast them down to hell, and delivered them into chains of darkness, to be reserved unto judgment;

God is using Hell as a place to hold these angels[5] until He is ready to judge them. Hell provided the perfect location for them. These angels were captured and delivered to Hell because of the sins they committed. They are being held in "chains of darkness", awaiting their judgment. They are fastened and secured in their cells by special chains that God had forged.[6] They are still there awaiting judgment.

Angels are not the only creatures confined to Hell. We also find the souls of men imprisoned there.

_____

[5] I believe these are the angels that sinned in the days of Noah.
Gen. 6:2 That the sons of God saw the daughters of men that they were fair; and they took them wives of all which they chose.
[6] Hell is a literal, physical place located in the center of the earth holding captive spiritual creatures. We are not told what God made the "chains of darkness" and "bars" out of, but we do know they perfectly perform the function for which God created them.

All the unrighteous, wicked of the earth find their place in Hell after they die.

Psa. 9:17 The wicked shall be turned into hell, and all the nations that forget God.

For the past 6,000 years, Hell has been the only destination for the unbelieving soul.

Hell is currently only occupied by unrighteous souls; but, there was a time when righteous men went there. Until God moved the location of Abraham's bosom (when Christ brought it into heaven after Calvary), the souls of righteous men also went to Hell. [7]

In Psalms 30, David, a righteous man, writes about going to Hell after he dies.

Psa. 30:9 What profit is there in my blood, when I go down to the pit? Shall the dust praise thee? shall it declare thy truth?

David was not the only righteous man who was confined to Hell, so was Abraham before him and Lazarus after him.

---

[7] Before Calvary, all men still had sin that was laid at their feet. Noah, Abraham, and David were still rightly accused of sin. No perfect sacrifice had yet been made that could take away their sin. God could not officially declare them righteous, for their sin still remained. God knew that one day a sufficient payment would be made, therefore He divided Hell into two compartments. He created the side of torment for the unrighteous and the paradise side for the righteous. God knew that in the future He would be able to declare them righteous so He allowed them to rest in paradise until the payment for their sin was made at Calvary.

Luk. 16:23 And in hell he lift up his eyes, being in torments, and seeth Abraham afar off, and Lazarus in his bosom.

Prior to the resurrection of Jesus Christ, all men, whether wicked or righteous, were placed into Hell. Hell was the prison for all men.

We must remember, that God divided Hell into two compartments. The torment side is where all the unrighteous souls go to await their final judgment. Abraham's bosom was where all the righteous souls went to await God's call.

CHAPTER 3

HOW DOES THE SOUL TRAVEL TO HELL?

What happens to the soul immediately upon death and how does it travel to Hell?

While man is alive, he chooses where he wants to go and when he wants to go there. It is up to him, he makes the choice; he is free. This all changes when he dies. At death, God takes control of the soul.

Eze. 18:4 Behold, all souls are mine; as the soul of the father, so also the soul of the son is mine: the soul that sinneth, it shall die.

At death, the soul of the righteous and unrighteous is in God's hands. The soul is now His possession, to do with as His word reveals. The soul of the saved and unsaved is fully subject to the will of God. This is a blessing for the saved, but to the lost, the Bible says;

Heb. 10:31 It is a fearful thing to fall into the hands of the living God.

This truth should cause the lost to accept God's salvation.

God has prepared one way for a righteous person, and another way for an unrighteous person to travel to Hell. We will first look at how a righteous person traveled to Hell before the cross.

- The Righteous -

Num. 27:13 And when thou hast seen it, thou also shalt be gathered unto thy people, as Aaron thy brother was gathered.

2 Chr. 34:28 Behold, I will gather thee to thy fathers, and thou shalt be gathered to thy grave in peace, neither shall thine eyes see all the evil that I will bring upon this place, and upon the inhabitants of the same. So they brought the king word again.[8]

In these verses God was speaking to righteous men, Moses and Hilkiah. God promised to "gather" the righteous souls together.

The scriptures tell us how God gathers the righteous souls.

Luk. 16:22a And it came to pass, that the beggar died, and was carried by the angels into Abraham's bosom:

We see angels carrying Lazarus to Abraham's bosom. One of the jobs of the angels was to help with the gathering of the righteous souls. Angels were in charge of transporting these righteous souls to Hell. At death, angels would meet the soul as it departed from the body and guide the soul to Hell. They actually carried the soul.

This is a wonderful display of God's love toward the righteous. At the moment of death, the righteous

---

[8] We see the soul of King Hilkiah being "gathered" to his fathers, and the physical body is "gathered" to the grave. This beautifully shows the distinction between the soul and the body.

encountered God's care and comfort producing joy and peace for the newly departed. Death is not a thing to be feared as it provides a release from the groaning and travailing of this world into the arms of a loving God. [9]

- The Unrighteous -

When the unrighteous die they do not just appear in Hell, as many people believe. God has established a mechanism to move the soul from the dead body and deliver it to Hell. The journey for an unrighteous soul is quite the opposite from the righteous.

Luk. 16:22b the rich man also died, and was buried;

When we look at the unrighteous rich man we see a different scenario. He is not gathered; there are no angels present to help him. No, he is left alone, to journey to Hell by himself. We find out more about the journey of the unrighteous from Job.

Job revealed what happened to the unrighteous soul, "the rich man" at death. Job described the frightening journey the "rich man" took to Hell.

Job 27:19-23 The rich man shall lie down, but he shall not be gathered: he openeth his eyes, and he is not. Terrors take hold on him as waters, a tempest stealeth him away in the night.

---

[9]Today in the dispensation of the grace of God, when a righteous person dies, they immediately go to be with the Lord in heaven.
2 Cor. 5:8 We are confident, I say, and willing rather to be absent from the body, and to be present with the Lord.

The east wind carrieth him away, and he departeth: and as a storm hurleth him out of his place. For God shall cast upon him, and not spare: he would fain flee out of his hand. Men shall clap their hands at him, and shall hiss him out of his place.

In verse 19 we see the rich man "lie down", this means that he had died.[10] The unrighteous will "not be gathered". God does not send angels to comfort, guide, or carry the soul. The unrighteous are left alone and unaided on their journey to Hell.

Job 27:19b he openeth his eyes, and he is not.

The moment this rich man died, his soul left his body. When the scriptures state, "he openeth his eyes" it is referring to the eyes of the soul.[11] The eyes of his physical body are closed because they are dead, but his soul is alive and can see.

The scriptures then state, "and he is not", this is teaching us that the soul knows that it has just been released from the body through death. The soul can see the dead body from which it just departed. The soul knows that the body it once inhabited is now dead; it "is not". This is the first thought of the soul; it knows it has just been released from the physical body through death. The soul

---

[10] Job uses the same wording when talking about his own death.
Job 14:12-13 So man lieth down, and riseth not: till the heavens be no more, they shall not awake, nor be raised out of their sleep.

[11] More will be discussed about the opening of the soul in Chapter 6.

is conscious, can think, comprehend, and is aware of its surroundings.

Job 27: 20 Terrors take hold on him as waters, a tempest stealeth him away in the night.

The soul is naked and stripped of all that the physical world provides. The words, "terrors take hold of him" teach that the soul is terrorized, frightened, and horrified as it comes to grips with this new reality of death. But there is something even more terrifying that the soul experiences. It feels a wind, a temptatious wind. This "tempest" has strong winds that start to drive the soul away from the body. The frightening sound of the wind causes the soul to shake with fear. The soul is terrified as it is caught in the "tempest" and thrown. This tempest is called the "east wind".[12]

Job 27: 21 The east wind carrieth him away, and he departeth: and as a storm hurleth him out of his place.

The scriptures state that there is a wind, an "east wind". This wind is in the spiritual world and comes upon all the unrighteous souls of the earth at death. This "east wind" is a "tempest", a storm that "hurleth him out of his place". This wind is as a violent storm that snatches the soul and causes it to be thrown. The "tempest" "hurleth" the soul from the place of death. The soul is powerless against this wind; it cannot stand against it. This is a terrifying experience. This storm causes the soul to "depart", to leave the land of the living and start the journey toward Hell.

---

[12] See appendix, "The East Wind"

34

Job also mentions "waters", that "take hold on him". These "waters" will be described shortly. The fear that is experienced by the soul is the same fear as one would experience when drowning. Drowning is a most frightening experience, the gasping for breath, the water covering the head, fighting to reach the surface. God's wrath is beginning to be poured out on the unrighteous. God created this storm to catch all the unrighteous souls of men. **God is not mocked, He will repay the wicked for their evil ways and it starts at the moment of death with this tempest.**

Men think they can escape the wrath of God; but they will not. They will not be able to flee "out of his hand". Men may try to run and hide from God, but it will be useless. There is no place to go. God has prepared a storm, the "east wind" to collect all the souls of unrighteous men.

God is a loving and gracious God; however, He is also just. He will judge those who refuse to believe His word. God will pour out His wrath and fury upon all the souls of unrighteous men. **This wrath starts the moment the unrighteous die.**

**Psa. 73:18-19 Surely thou didst set them in slippery places: thou castedst them down into destruction.
How are they brought into desolation, as in a moment! they are utterly consumed with terrors.**

The souls of the dead cannot stay to haunt, talk with, or commune with any other beings; they are all hurled out of their place "in a moment".[13]

---

[13]Those who claim to of had an afterlife experience are confused or lying. The descriptions that they give of seeing warm bright lights,

They are "utterly consumed with terrors". Every aspect of their being is assaulted by God's wrath. The sights they see are terrifying, the feelings they have are horrible, and the thoughts they have are full of fright. There is no part of them that is not experiencing God's terror. It pours into every member of their soul.

We are reminded of the verse in Hebrews referring to the unrighteous.

Heb. 10:31 It is a fearful thing to fall into the hands of the living God.

It is frightening and terrifying for the soul of the unrighteous as they start to experience the wrath of God. The soul is consumed with terror. This will happen to every unrighteous soul. No matter how proud, strong, or confident they were in life, they will all be consumed with terror as they start on the path toward Hell.

Job 27:22 For God shall cast upon him, and not spare: he would fain flee out of his hand.

Psa. 73:18b thou castedst them down into destruction.

God is casting these souls away. God forcibly and violently drives the souls of unrighteous men down into Hell. God thrusts these souls out of the land of the living, rejected and alone. These souls have rejected the love of

---

friendly faces, God, or any other imaginations are evil and in opposition to the word of God. Experience is never to replace the revealed word of God.
2 Cor. 5:7 (For we walk by faith, not by sight:)

God; so, now they will justly experience the wrath of an angry God.

The scriptures reveal more about the descent of the unrighteous into Hell.

There are many passages in Psalms that talk about the events of the cross and what took place after it. When Christ died, He went to Hell.[14] Christ became sin for us; therefore, it was necessary that His soul experience the same wrath of God as would any unrighteous man.

Isa. 53:10a Yet it pleased the LORD to bruise him; he hath put him to grief: when thou shalt make his soul an offering for sin,

In the following verses we see what happened to the Lord Jesus Christ immediately after He died. These verses are the direct account of the Lord Jesus Christ describing His descent into Hell.[15]

Psa. 42:5-7 Why art thou cast down, O my soul? and why art thou disquieted in me? hope thou in God: for I shall yet praise him for the help of his countenance.
O my God, my soul is cast down within me: therefore will I remember thee from the land of Jordan, and of the Hermonites, from the hill Mizar.
Deep calleth unto deep at the noise of thy waterspouts: all thy waves and thy billows are gone over me.

---

[14] Discussed in chapter 8.
[15] Many Psalms are prophetic in nature and provide the thoughts, prayers, and activities of the Lord Jesus Christ.

Psa. 69:1-2 Save me, O God; for the waters are come in unto my soul.
I sink in deep mire, where there is no standing: I am come into deep waters, where the floods overflow me.

The Lord Jesus Christ talked about "waters"; these are the same "waters" that the rich man experienced in Job 27:20.

Job 27: 20a Terrors take hold on him as waters,

These "waters" are "deep waters" that come "unto the soul". As the soul is hurled by the east wind toward Hell, it will first go through water, encountering the "waves" and "billows". The soul will be sucked down into the terrifying waters. As the soul plummets into the waters, the waters will go "over", drowning the sinking soul.

At the bottom of the waters the soul will encounter "mire"; which can be best described as thick, wet clay.[16] The soul will begin to sink into this "mire". The foot will look for a place to stand upon, for a rock to hold itself up, but to no avail, "there is no standing". This mire is suffocating and frightening as one sinks deeper and deeper into it.

We see this "mire" mentioned again in Psalms 69.

Psa. 69:14-15 Deliver me out of the mire, and let me not sink: let me be delivered from them that hate me,

---

[16] **Psa. 40:2 He brought me up also out of an horrible pit, out of the miry clay, and set my feet upon a rock, and established my goings.**

and out of the deep waters.
Let not the waterflood overflow me, neither let the
deep swallow me up, and let not the pit shut her
mouth upon me.

This passage is again dealing with the Lord Jesus Christ as He sank into Hell. Notice how He is sinking into the "mire" that is in the "deep waters".

Psalms 69:15 gives a concise description of the path to Hell. First the soul is "overflowed" with water. As it drowns it comes to the "deep", which is where the "mire" is. After the "mire", Hell can be seen with its "mouth" opened to receive the soul.

We see these "waters" and the "waves" in the account of Jonah. In the case of Jonah, we have a righteous man being chastised of the Lord to bring him into a place of obedience.   God brought him through the same experience as an unrighteous man, as seen in the following verses.

Jon. 2:2-6 And said, I cried by reason of mine
affliction unto the LORD, and he heard me; out of the
belly of hell cried I, and thou heardest my voice.
For thou hadst cast me into the deep, in the midst of
the seas; and the floods compassed me about: all thy
billows and thy waves passed over me.
Then I said, I am cast out of thy sight; yet I will look
again toward thy holy temple.
The waters compassed me about, even to the soul:
the depth closed me round about, the weeds were
wrapped about my head.
I went down to the bottoms of the mountains; the
earth with her bars was about me for ever: yet hast

thou brought up my life from corruption, O LORD my God.

Jonah uses the same words to describe his journey as the Psalmist used of the Lord Jesus Christ in Psa. 42:7, "all thy billows and thy waves passed over me." This is showing how they both experienced the same thing. Notice how the "waters compassed" the "soul" of Jonah, then the mire of the "depth closed" about him. He finally reaches the location of Hell at the bottom of the mountains where he sees the bars of Hell.

Hell becomes visible as the soul sinks through the "mire". It is seen under all the mountains. The bars of Hell are visible in every direction. The "mouth" of Hell is then seen.

Psa. 69:15 Let not the waterflood overflow me, neither let the deep swallow me up, and let not the pit shut her mouth upon me.

The "mouth" opens to swallow the soul. This is a most frightening sight, seeing the gate of Hell open to receive the soul. The closing of the "mouth" behind the soul seals the doom and the reality of hopelessness sets in. Hopeless and terrified, the unrighteous soul has now arrived in Hell.

The scriptures present a terrifying journey for the unrighteous soul going to Hell.

A: The eyes of the soul open as it leaves the body.

B: The soul is conscious as it departs the body.

C: An east wind comes as a tempest and hurls
            the soul away.

D: The tempest sucks the soul downward into
            the earth through a watery pathway.

E: The soul is overflowed with water as it
            goes downward.

F: The soul encounters the deep or miry clay
            and sinks into it.

G: The soul sees the bottoms of the
            mountains.
H: The soul sees the bars of Hell.

I: The soul sees the mouth of Hell open.

J: The soul enters Hell and the mouth shuts
            behind it.

This is a most horrific and frightening journey that
happens to all the unrighteous the moment death occurs.
The soul goes through this traumatic and terrifying
process alone and rejected of God.[17]

---

[17] "Knowing the terror of the Lord" as it is executed on the
unrighteous, saints should have a heart for the souls of men.
**2 Cor. 6:2 (For he saith, I have heard thee in a time accepted, and
in the day of salvation have I succoured thee: behold, now is the
accepted time; behold, now is the day of salvation.)**
"Now is the day of salvation" to escape the damnation of God.
**Heb. 2:3 How shall we escape, if we neglect so great salvation;
which at the first began to be spoken by the Lord, and was
confirmed unto us by them that heard him;**

CHAPTER 4

THE ACTIVITY OF THE SOULS IN HELL

- The Worm -

Prior to discussing what the souls do in Hell; we need to understand some things about the soul.

The soul inhabits the physical body before death. At death, the soul leaves the body.

Job tells us what happens to the soul as it leaves the body.

Job 27:19 The rich man shall lie down, but he shall not be gathered: he openeth his eyes, and he is not.

In the above verse Job describes the death of the rich man. We have learned that as the soul departs from the physical body the "eyes" of the soul "openeth". Job is teaching us that the soul has eyes. While the soul is in the physical body the eyes of the soul are closed. This is because the soul can see through the physical eyes of the body. It is through the members of the physical body (eyes, ears, nose, etc...) that the soul can see, feel, taste, touch, move, etc...

We know, that when the soul has left the body at death, it is capable of touching, tasting, hearing, moving, etc... This is seen in the account of the rich man and Lazarus, we learn that the soul could hear, feel, and taste. The soul also has a tongue on which it sought water and the soul can move from one place to another. This is teaching us that the soul has other members, such as ears, nose, and tongue that can interact with the environment besides the eyes. These members of the soul are closed, like the eyes, while in the physical body.

When the soul leaves the body, all the members of the soul open to provide what the physical body used to. The eyes will open as well as the ears, nose, mouth, and all the other members of the soul. The soul will be as alert to its surroundings as it was in the physical body. The soul moves seamlessly out of the physical body at death, yet retaining its ability to sense and interact with its environment as its members open. This all happens immediately at death.

The souls are recognizable to one another through identifiable characteristics that remain with the soul. They know who they are seeing.

We also know that the soul is conscious and that it can think and reason. The soul retains its memory and can learn, as seen in Luke 16. The rich man knew who Abraham was when he saw him. Abraham was able to learn about the lives of the rich man and Lazarus when they were on the earth.

The scriptures call the form of the soul of both the righteous and unrighteous, a "worm".

Job. 25:6 How much less man, that is a worm? and the son of man, which is a worm?

In the above verse Job describes man as a "worm". Jesus Christ also describes Himself as a "worm" after His soul left His body at the cross.

Psa. 22:6 But I am a worm, and no man; a reproach of men, and despised of the people.

Jesus Christ refers to all the souls in Hell as "worms".

Mar. 9:43-44 And if thy hand offend thee, cut it off: it is better for thee to enter into life maimed, than having two hands to go into hell, into the fire that never shall be quenched:
Where their worm dieth not, and the fire is not quenched.

Isaiah also calls those in Hell, "worms".

Isa. 14:11 Thy pomp is brought down to the grave, and the noise of thy viols: the worm is spread under thee, and the worms cover thee.

The "worms" in the above verse are the souls of those in Hell.

In Mark 9:43 we learn that the "worm dieth not". The soul or "worm" is eternal. It cannot die or cease to exist. It will survive all of eternity, never to perish or be annihilated. It "dieth not".

- The Activity of the Righteous -

We will now look at what the righteous souls did in Hell.

Luk. 16: 25 But Abraham said, Son, remember that thou in thy lifetime receivedst thy good things, and likewise Lazarus evil things: but now he is comforted, and thou art tormented.

The righteous souls that are placed into Abraham's bosom are at rest. They are comforted. They are not terrified or frightened. Life in "paradise" is exactly that, a life of ease and comfort. The scriptures tell us more about the activities in Abraham's bosom.

Job described what he was planning on doing in Hell when he gets there.

Job 14:12-15 So man lieth down, and riseth not: till the heavens be no more, they shall not awake, nor be raised out of their sleep.
O that thou wouldest hide me in the grave, that thou wouldest keep me secret, until thy wrath be past, that thou wouldest appoint me a set time, and remember me!
If a man die, shall he live again? all the days of my appointed time will I wait, till my change come.
Thou shalt call, and I will answer thee: thou wilt have a desire to the work of thine hands.

Job was speaking about his own death when he stated, "so a man lieth down, and riseth not". He knew his physical body would "sleep"[18] and that it would not be awakened/resurrected until "the heavens be no more".

Job wanted God to hide his body in the grave, while his soul went to Hell.

---

[18] See appendix, "The Grave".

He knew he would die one day and then he proceeded to describe what he would do after he died. He knew his time in Hell would be "till the heavens be no more". Job knew that God had an appointed time for him to be resurrected.

Job then asked that God would put him in a "secret" place. This secret place was in Hell. He asked for this because he knew God would one day pour out His "wrath" and Job hoped to escape this wrath. Job trusted that God would hide him from the wrath to come.

Job asked God to put him in a secret place because he knew he could not do it himself. God must put Job in a "secret" place where His wrath will not go. [19]

Job sought to be hid until God's wrath is past. He then looked for God to "remember me!" Job knew there was an "appointed", "set time" when God would remember him.

Job knew he would live again. Job is not questioning his resurrection when he says, "If a man die, shall he live again?" This is a rhetorical question with the answer being; Yes! Job looked forward to the day of his resurrection, he knew it was going to happen.

Job 19:26 And though after my skin worms destroy this body, yet in my flesh shall I see God:

---

[19] The "workers of iniquity" are the unrighteous, they may try and hide but God will find them. There is no place for the wicked to "hide" from God. There is no "secret" place for them to flee. They will feel the full force of God's wrath.

Job 34:22 There is no darkness, nor shadow of death, where the workers of iniquity may hide themselves.

The resurrection would be according to God's timing. Until that time Job would "wait". Job understood that after he died, God would place him in a safe, "secret" place and once there, Job would "wait" for the resurrection. He would "wait" until the "appointed time", a special day set by God.

Job also stated that while he waited, he would be listening for something. Job knew he would be awake and conscious after death. Job would have to be, in order to be able to listen. Job knew this to be true and thus Job stated he would spend his time listening. But what was he listening for? He was listening for the "call" of God. Job knew God would "call" for him after God's wrath had passed. God will not forget the righteous; He will not leave them without hope. Job understood all of this. He knew God would "call" for him and resurrect him at a "set time", but until that time, Job was planning on waiting and listening for God's "call".

We have learned that in Abraham's bosom, the righteous souls "wait" and listen for the "call" of God. They are waiting for a "set time" when God would "call" them to the resurrection.

We can also learn more about the activities of the righteous in Hell from Abel. When Cain killed Abel, Abel's soul went to Abraham's bosom, the paradise side of Hell. As we have learned, that is where the souls of the righteous went prior to Calvary. Abraham's bosom was empty at this time and Abel was the first man to inhabit it. The Lord tells us what Abel was doing in paradise when God confronted Cain for his murder.

Gen. 4:10 And he said, What hast thou done? the voice of thy brother's blood crieth unto me from the ground.

Abel's voice still cried, even after his physical death. Abel could speak from Hell. The scriptures state that he "crieth unto" God. Abel was crying out to God for justice, he was crying against his brother who murdered him. Abel was not silenced in death, he could still speak, he could still cry unto God for justice. God heard and continues to hear the cries of the righteous souls. The cries are for vengeance against those who persecuted the righteous; God hears these cries and will answer in His own time.

Rom. 12:19 Dearly beloved, avenge not yourselves, but rather give place unto wrath: for it is written, Vengeance is mine; I will repay, saith the Lord.

- The Activity of the Unrighteous -

We will now look at what happens to the unrighteous in the torment side of Hell. The torment side of Hell is hot with flames leaping at those who find their residency there. This tormenting flame only gets hotter as one goes deeper and deeper into the lower levels of Hell.

Luk. 16:24 And he cried and said, Father Abraham, have mercy on me, and send Lazarus, that he may dip the tip of his finger in water, and cool my tongue;

The rich man saw the water on the other side of the gulf. He wanted some. He cries, he cries for water, if only one drop of it.[20]

The lack of water, or any comforts cause those to cry, to cry for some sort of relief; but, it will not be found. The moans and cries of the unrighteous souls echo across the stony interior of Hell. The rich man was probably not the only one begging for water to be brought to him, but maybe billions upon billions of souls stand on the edge of the abyss, crying out for water.[21]

Psa. 116:3 The sorrows of death compassed me, and the pains of hell gat hold upon me: I found trouble and sorrow.

These pains "hold" unto the souls, they do not leave them. Every moment is spent in agony, suffering, and hurting. "Trouble" and "sorrow" are relentless.

2 Sam. 22:6 The sorrows of hell compassed me about; the snares of death prevented me;

Hell is a place of sorrows and encompasses all those within its confines with sorrow. There is no joy to be found, no happiness or jubilation on this side of Hell.

---

[20]In the land of the living, the Lord shares His goodness with all men, both the righteous and unrighteous.
Act. 14:17 Nevertheless he left not himself without witness, in that he did good, and gave us rain from heaven, and fruitful seasons, filling our hearts with food and gladness.
God's goodness is removed from those who die in unbelief.
[21]The account of the rich man and Lazarus is to cause men to fear God, tremble at His word, and bring them to salvation. The unbeliever who mocks and scoffs has this to look forward to.

They don't have the strength to change their condition or circumstances.

Psa. 88:4 I am counted with them that go down into the pit: I am as a man that hath no strength:

They no longer possess the strength they once had in life. They have become weak and powerless. They cannot stop the flames, they cannot cross the gulf, and they cannot escape Hell. They truly have no strength.

God damns the souls found on the torment side of Hell.

Mat. 23:33 Ye serpents, ye generation of vipers, how can ye escape the damnation of hell?

God's damning includes His silence as noted by David in Psalms.

Psa. 28:1 Unto thee will I cry, O LORD my rock; be not silent to me: lest, if thou be silent to me, I become like them that go down into the pit.

God does not speak to those in "the pit", Hell. He is "silent" to those on the torment side.

The unrighteous are damned by God to await their final judgment. The souls are damned to an existence of pain, wailing, and suffering.

The scriptures teach of a social order in Hell for the unrighteous.

Isa. 14:18 All the kings of the nations, even all of them, lie in glory, every one in his own house.

In this verse, Isaiah is talking about unrighteous men in Hell. We see that when an unrighteous king dies, he will go to "his own house". This sheds light on the social structure in Hell. These "houses" are not literal buildings, but instead refer to members of a family by lineage, race, or ancestry. This verse teaches that when the unjust dies and arrives in Hell, they will seek to find those they know, their family. There will be a reuniting of family members in Hell, but this will not be a joyous event. Each new arrival will be met with moans and sorrow from their fellow family members.

These "houses" are not limited to one's family but also relate to one's nationality. The souls in Hell also band together by their nationality or kingdom they belonged to on the earth. We will see more on this shortly in the next few verses.

The scriptures say that these kings have a "glory" in Hell. But what exactly does this mean? We know this does not mean that they have riches, comforts, or even water. But what they do retain is their social power; they remain as kings, authority figures, presidents, dictators, emperors, rulers, etc... Those whom they ruled over in life will look upon them as rulers in Hell.

Isa. 14:9 Hell from beneath is moved for thee to meet thee at thy coming: it stirreth up the dead for thee, even all the chief ones of the earth; it hath raised up from their thrones all the kings of the nations.

The scriptures talk about the "chief ones" and "kings of the nations" who rise from "their thrones". These thrones are in Hell. This is teaching us that there is a social and political structure in Hell. The "kings", or "chief ones of the earth" who died will once again seek to reign in Hell. In Hell they will seek the same "thrones" or authority they had in the land of the living.

Ezekiel writes about many earthly kingdoms that ceased in the land of the living but continue in Hell. Each kingdom amassed around their "king".

Eze. 32:22-23 Asshur is there and all her company: his graves are about him: all of them slain, fallen by the sword:
Whose graves are set in the sides of the pit, and her company is round about her grave: all of them slain, fallen by the sword, which caused terror in the land of the living.

The kingdom of Asshur occupies a place in Hell. The "fallen" are "round about", the dead have gathered together around their once famous kingdom. Their "terror in the land of the living" is over, but now they wallow in pain together in Hell. The same is true of the nation of Elam. We see them all gathered around their king.

Eze. 32:29-30 There is Elam and all her multitude round about her grave, all of them slain, fallen by the sword, which are gone down uncircumcised into the nether parts of the earth, which caused their terror in the land of the living; yet have they borne their shame with them that go down to the pit.
They have set her a bed in the midst of the slain with all her multitude: her graves are round about him: all of them uncircumcised, slain by the sword: though their terror was caused in the land of the living, yet

have they borne their shame with them that go down to the pit: he is put in the midst of them that be slain.

The nation of Elam once "caused terror in the land of the living", but now they are in "the pit" or Hell. The souls of this once great nation have gathered "round about him", their king.

The same is true of the nation of Meshech, Tubal.

Eze. 32:27-28 There is Meshech, Tubal, and all her multitude: her graves are round about him: all of them uncircumcised, slain by the sword, though they caused their terror in the land of the living.
And they shall not lie with the mighty that are fallen of the uncircumcised, which are gone down to hell with their weapons of war: and they have laid their swords under their heads, but their iniquities shall be upon their bones, though they were the terror of the mighty in the land of the living.

There is also Edom.

Eze. 32:29 There is Edom, her kings, and all her princes, which with their might are laid by them that were slain by the sword: they shall lie with the uncircumcised, and with them that go down to the pit.

There are the nations of the north, even the Zidonians.

Eze. 32:30 There be the princes of the north, all of them, and all the Zidonians, which are gone down with the slain; with their terror they are ashamed of their might; and they lie uncircumcised with them

that be slain by the sword, and bear their shame with them that go down to the pit.

In fact, all nations will be found in Hell, each gathered together around their leaders. There you will find Hitler with his Nazi party around him. Ganges Kuhn is there with the Mongols as well as Nero and the Romans of his day. Each "chief one of the earth" enthroned, each one usurping authority, and each one attempting to rule over others in Hell.

Everyone is in torment; no one is without pain and suffering. These "kings" and "chief ones of the earth" are suffering the same as those that have gathered around them. The social order found in Hell will abruptly end when God calls them before the Great White Throne and cast them all into the Lake of Fire.

These nations and kings speak to one another. We see this with Pharaoh.

Eze. 32:18 Son of man, wail for the multitude of Egypt, and cast them down, even her, and the daughters of the famous nations, unto the nether parts of the earth, with them that go down into the pit.

Eze. 32:21 The strong among the mighty shall speak to him out of the midst of hell with them that help him: they are gone down, they lie uncircumcised, slain by the sword.

Eze. 32:31 Pharaoh shall see them, and shall be comforted over all his multitude, even Pharaoh and all his army slain by the sword, saith the Lord GOD.

54

From the above verses we see Pharaoh being "cast" down to "the pit". The "strong among the mighty" speak to him, these are the leaders of other nations; they will speak to Pharaoh in Hell. He is able to see the other nations and their kings. He is able to converse with them.

As Pharaoh looks at the other nations the scriptures state that Pharaoh is "comforted". But what does this mean, for there is no escaping the flame of torment? When Pharaoh compares his nation to that of the other "kings" he finds "comfort" in that his nation was one of the stronger ones. He shall look at the multitude that went with him to Hell and find "comfort" in how many souls he leads. His nation was truly one of the stronger ones on the earth compared to those he sees in Hell. This is truly evil and sickening, that Pharaoh will take pleasure and "comfort" in that he led so many into Hell with him.[22]

We have seen that there are kings, thrones, and nations in Hell. These nations take up residency in the sides of the pit.

These "sides of the pit" house the nations and kings and their thrones. If one were to walk down Hell, you would

---

[22] There will be many evil and corrupt men in Hell who in life knowingly deceived and blinded the eyes of the lost to the gospel of Christ. They will take "pleasure" is seeing these souls in Hell. These are religious men who walked in the "way of Cain". Read the author's book on the subject, "The Way Of Cain – The Creation Of Man's Religion".
Mat. 23:15 Woe unto you, scribes and Pharisees, hypocrites! for ye compass sea and land to make one proselyte, and when he is made, ye make him twofold more the child of hell than yourselves.

see chambers in the sides of Hell; there each nation would be together around their leader.

We can see a similarity between the social order of Hell and that of today's prisons. When a new inmate is delivered he is at first alone. The inmate looks around and immediately tries to link up with anyone he may know. They may try and find a family member incarcerated there, a friend, or even members of their gang. Many prisons have the same gangs within them that exist on the outside of the prison. Leaders who led gangs on the outside of prison continue as leaders when incarcerated in prison. This is also true of Hell.

One reason souls band together in Hell is because Hell is not a friendly place. Let's go back to the "rich man" described by Job. We already saw his journey to Hell, but Job also described what happens to him in Hell.

Job 27:23 Men shall clap their hands at him, and shall hiss him out of his place.

Here we see that men "clap their hands at him" and they "hiss" at him. This activity is happening in Hell. When this man entered Hell, the occupants harassed and mocked him. They verbally insulted and shouted at him. They looked upon him with evil and pushed him around. This same activity takes place in prisons today. When a new inmate enters the prison the others immediately look him upon. They may jeer, shout, or even toss things at him. This is not a friendly welcoming greeting, but a frightening one. This harassing may continue as long as the inmate is in prison.

The "rich man" in Job found a "place" to hide and get away from the jeering. This "place" he had found did not last long. The mobs that roam Hell found him and hissed "him out of his place". They sought him and found him, they did not allow the rich man to rest or get away from their abuse. This "rich man" has no "place" and must constantly be on the move, constantly trying to find another place. This "rich man" is not the only person who is hounded and abused by other "prisoners" in Hell.

There is no hope for those found on the torment side of Hell.

Isa. 38:18 For the grave cannot praise thee, death can not celebrate thee: they that go down into the pit cannot hope for thy truth.

1 The. 4:13 But I would not have you to be ignorant, brethren, concerning them which are asleep, that ye sorrow not, even as others which have no hope.

The "worms" will wait in the tormenting flame until they are judged of God. They have no hope, no reprieve, and no escape from the wrath of God.

CHAPTER 5

SATAN AND HELL

When discussing Hell there is one figure who is associated with it more than any other, and that is the Devil. Most of the world believes in a Devil and that his residence is in Hell. But what do the scriptures say concerning the Devil, his abode, and his relation to Hell?

- Satan and His Realm -

The scriptures state that God created a beautiful creature in Ezekiel.

Eze. 28:14-15 Thou art the anointed cherub that covereth; and I have set thee so: thou wast upon the holy mountain of God; thou hast walked up and down in the midst of the stones of fire.
Thou wast perfect in thy ways from the day that thou wast created, till iniquity was found in thee.

God created a most wonderful creature. This creature was a cherub, a special class of beings that surrounded God's throne. It was this cherub's job to cover the throne of God, to stand over it. This creature was perfect until "iniquity was found" in him.

Isa. 14: 12-17 How art thou fallen from heaven, O Lucifer, son of the morning! how art thou cut down to the ground, which didst weaken the nations!
For thou hast said in thine heart, I will ascend into heaven, I will exalt my throne above the stars of God:

I will sit also upon the mount of the congregation, in the sides of the north:
I will ascend above the heights of the clouds; I will be like the most High.
Yet thou shalt be brought down to hell, to the sides of the pit.
They that see thee shall narrowly look upon thee, and consider thee, saying, Is this the man that made the earth to tremble, that did shake kingdoms;
That made the world as a wilderness, and destroyed the cities thereof; that opened not the house of his prisoners?

This creature sinned and fell from its position of covering the throne of God. He wanted to be God. We read in Isaiah 14:12, that his name is Lucifer. Lucifer is also called by many other names such as Satan, Devil, and the great dragon.

According to the scriptures, God prepared the "everlasting fire", Lake of Fire, for Satan's ultimate punishment.

Mat. 25:41 Then shall he say also unto them on the left hand, Depart from me, ye cursed, into everlasting fire, prepared for the devil and his angels:

Rev. 20:10 And the devil that deceived them was cast into the lake of fire and brimstone, where the beast and the false prophet are, and shall be tormented day and night for ever and ever.

The Lake of Fire is not Hell. These are two separate and distinct places of torment. More will be said about the Lake of Fire in chapter 12.

The Lake of Fire has been prepared for Satan, but he is not there yet. So the question is, where is Satan now?

Satan is the "god of this world".

2 Cor. 4:4 In whom the god of this world hath blinded the minds of them which believe not, lest the light of the glorious gospel of Christ, who is the image of God, should shine unto them

As the "god of this world", Satan is free to roam wherever he wants. He roams in the earth and in heaven.

Peter states that Satan walks the earth.

1 Pet. 5:8 Be sober, be vigilant; because your adversary the devil, as a roaring lion, walketh about, seeking whom he may devour:

Satan was on the earth during the time of our Lord Jesus Christ's earthly ministry.

Luk. 4:5-6 And the devil, taking him up into an high mountain, shewed unto him all the kingdoms of the world in a moment of time.
And the devil said unto him, All this power will I give thee, and the glory of them: for that is delivered unto me; and to whomsoever I will I give it.

Satan is not limited to the earth. Satan can roam the heavens, as seen when he presented himself before the Lord in the heavens as described by Job.

Job 1:6-7 Now there was a day when the sons of God came to present themselves before the LORD, and Satan came also among them.
And the LORD said unto Satan, Whence comest thou? Then Satan answered the LORD, and said, From going to and fro in the earth, and from walking up and down in it.

From the above passages we know that Satan has liberty to roam the earth and heavens. He moves freely between heaven and earth. Knowing that Satan is not bound or incarcerated, but is free to move as he wishes, we know that Satan is not being held in Hell. Satan is not from Hell nor is he being held in Hell. Hell is not Satan's home.

Just because Hell is not the home of Satan does not mean that Satan is not interested in it. Satan takes advantage of the existence of Hell and is actively involved with its operations. More will be said about this later.

We must first look at one of Satan's primary roles, that of a lawyer.

- Satan the Prosecutor -

Rev. 12:10 And I heard a loud voice saying in heaven, Now is come salvation, and strength, and the kingdom of our God, and the power of his Christ: for the accuser of our brethren is cast down, which accused them before our God day and night.

Satan is the "accuser of our brethren" in this verse. He accuses, lays blame against, and brings legal charges against men. This is the activity of a courtroom prosecutor.

We see the courtroom of heaven in Zechariah. There is a prosecutor and a defendant who stand before the judge. The prosecutor is on the right side of the defendant.

Zec. 3:1 And he shewed me Joshua the high priest standing before the angel of the LORD, and Satan standing at his right hand to resist him.

In this verse we see Joshua and Satan standing before the LORD, who is the Judge. Satan, the prosecutor, is standing at the "right hand" of Joshua. Amazingly, our own courtrooms are modeled after this. The defendant and prosecutor stand before a judge, with the prosecutor at the right hand of the defendant.

As a prosecutor, Satan prosecutes all men. Satan uses the Law of Moses to charge all men as lawbreakers. Even though the law was only given to Israel, God wrote the "work of the law" in the hearts of the gentiles.

Rom. 2:15a Which shew the work of the law written in their hearts,

Everyone knows what God's laws are. Men know what God says is right or wrong because God wrote it in the hearts of every person. No man can plead ignorance to God's law.

Satan knows that men break God's laws and he has taken it upon himself to accuse all men of violating them. He comes before God and accuses mankind of breaking the law.

In his role as prosecutor, Satan has become a great lawyer. Outside of God Himself, Satan is probably the best legal mind in the universe. Satan studied the law; he knows and quotes the scriptures. His knowledge of the law is unexcelled. This is necessary because Satan wants to charge every person with every possible offense. We will see why shortly.

In Rev. 20:10 we read that his activity as a prosecutor continues "day and night". This is a time consuming job; but it is one that Satan takes great pride in doing.

The question must be asked, why would Satan take on the role of a prosecutor? Why would he accuse mankind?

We find the answer in Genesis.

Gen. 3:15 And I will put enmity between thee and the woman, and between thy seed and her seed; it shall bruise thy head, and thou shalt bruise his heel.

God pronounced a judgment against Satan after Adam sinned. God said that a seed of Eve would one day bruise the head of Satan. Satan understood exactly what God said, that it would be a child of a woman that would destroy him.

Satan did not just sit back and do nothing in relation to God's promise of his defeat. Satan developed a plan to counter God's promise.

Satan determined that if he could condemn all of Eve's children to the wrath of God, (all her seed) then God's promise to destroy Satan could never be fulfilled. Satan set about to find fault with every man or woman born. He accuses them before God "day and night". With every child born, Satan set about to prove to God that all men were evil and worthy of God's condemnation.

Satan knew that God was a just God and that if men violated God's law, God would have to condemn them. Satan used God's attribute of justice to have God condemn all those who sinned, knowing that God could not let the unrighteous acts of men go unpunished.

Satan knew there was a place God would house those who were to be condemned. Satan knew Hell was this place. Satan set about to imprison all of mankind, to make them his prisoners in Hell. If Satan could imprison all of mankind and prove them deserving of God's wrath, then the promise of God could never be fulfilled. There would be no man born of Eve that could ever destroy him, for all of them would be imprisoned in Hell, justly condemned for breaking God's laws, and under the wrath of God. This was Satan's grand design to thwart God's promise of Gen. 3:15.

Thus with each person born, Satan sought to condemn all and send all to prison/Hell. Satan knew there was no escape from Hell. With all men imprisoned in Hell and under the wrath of God, Satan would show God a liar and unable to fulfill His promise of destroying him.

- Satan's Role with Hell -

We have seen that Satan is a lawyer, a prosecutor, and how he condemns all men to Hell. The scriptures shed additional light on Satan's role in Hell.

Isa. 14: 12&17 How art thou fallen from heaven, O Lucifer, son of the morning! how art thou cut down to the ground, which didst weaken the nations!

That made the world as a wilderness, and destroyed the cities thereof; that opened not the house of his prisoners?

These verses are talking about Satan, Lucifer. Notice the end of verse 17, when talking about Satan, it states the he would "open not the house of his prisoners". The "house" that is being talked about is Hell, and in Hell are "his prisoners". By prosecuting all of mankind and having them committed to Hell to await a final judgment, the scriptures state that those souls have become "his prisoners". He is the one who has accused them and made sure that they have all been prosecuted for breaking the law, thus God calls the souls in Hell, Satan's - "his prisoners".[23]

Notice how Isaiah describes those in Hell as "prisoners".

Isa. 42:7 To open the blind eyes, to bring out the prisoners from the prison, and them that sit in darkness out of the prison house.

Again in Isaiah, we see these souls "shut up" in the prison house.

Isa. 24:22 And they shall be gathered together, as prisoners are gathered in the pit, and shall be shut up in the prison, and after many days shall they be visited.

---

[23] Hell is God's prison, but in Isa. 14:17 we learn that the prisoners have become Satan's, because he is the one who has prosecuted them.

Job also uses the term "prisoners" to describe those who are in Hell.

Job 3:18 There the prisoners rest together; they hear not the voice of the oppressor.

All these are Satan's prisoners. They are kept there because they have violated the Law. They are all guilty and therefore rightly condemned. Satan uses the law to prove that each person has violated it. Since all men sin, Satan had been able to condemn all men, they cannot go free, they are his.

Isa. 14:17b that opened not the house of his prisoners?

Isaiah states that Satan "opened not the house". Until Calvary, Satan kept all the souls of men locked up in Hell. This means that Satan could have opened the doors of Hell but he chose not to. Satan was in a position to open the door or keep it closed. He would not open the gate of Hell and release them. If Satan could open or close the door he had to have the keys to Hell, for he would need the keys to open the door. We will see in a later chapter what has happened to these keys.

Satan is a prideful selfish creature only looking out for himself. He is not a friend of man nor is he seeking man's benefit. He only seeks to save himself and will damn all of mankind in the process.

CHAPTER 6

GOD'S RESPONSE

How was God going to fulfill His promise of Gen. 3:15 if every person was condemned to Hell? No one could defeat Satan if they were all imprisoned in Hell and under the wrath of God awaiting judgment.

All of Eve's children were incapable of defeating Satan because they were all consigned to Hell. Even though there were a few occasions where a soul returned from Hell to the land of the living, they each returned to Hell.

Jhn. 11:43-44 And when he thus had spoken, he cried with a loud voice, Lazarus, come forth.
And he that was dead came forth, bound hand and foot with graveclothes: and his face was bound about with a napkin. Jesus saith unto them, Loose him, and let him go.

1 Ki. 17:21 And he stretched himself upon the child three times, and cried unto the LORD, and said, O LORD my God, I pray thee, let this child's soul come into him again.

Lazarus and the child were brought back to life from Abraham's bosom but they both returned when they died. No mortal man, even if brought back from the dead, could destroy Satan because they were all sinners and under the wrath of God.

But God had a plan, in that He had promised a Saviour, Who would destroy Satan and his works according to Gen. 3:15.

The Lord Jesus Christ was this Saviour. Let's look at a conversation between the members of the Godhead as recorded in Hebrews.

Heb. 10:5-7 Wherefore when he cometh into the world, he saith, Sacrifice and offering thou wouldest not, but a body hast thou prepared me:
In burnt offerings and sacrifices for sin thou hast had no pleasure.
Then said I, Lo, I come in the volume of the book it is written of me, to do thy will, O God.

"When he cometh into the world" takes us back to the time when Jesus Christ was about to leave heaven and become a man. Jesus Christ speaks in verse 7, "Then said I". Christ came to do the will of God, to fulfill the promise in Gen. 3:15.

One of the purposes of the Lord's coming was to defeat Satan and to destroy his works.

1 Jhn. 3:8b For this purpose the Son of God was manifested, that he might destroy the works of the devil.

Jesus Christ was made the seed of the woman.

Gal. 4:4 But when the fulness of the time was come, God sent forth his Son, made of a woman, made under the law,

Jesus Christ had to become a man in order to fulfill the promise of Gen. 3:15. This was accomplished through the Holy Spirit creating a special body in Mary's womb.

Heb. 10:5 Wherefore when he cometh into the world, he saith, Sacrifice and offering thou wouldest not, but a body hast thou prepared me:

This body combined God and man together. In this "body" Jesus Christ was all God and all man. Only God could create such a "body", it was truly miraculous. Jesus never stopped being God when He became man.

With the birth of Christ, the stage was set for a battle between God's anointed Saviour and Satan.

CHAPTER 7

JESUS CHRIST VS. SATAN

Jesus Christ was born as the promised Seed of Gen. 3:15.

Luk. 2:11 For unto you is born this day in the city of David a Saviour, which is Christ the Lord.

When Satan realized that the promised Seed had entered the world he tried to kill Him. Satan thought that if he could kill Christ, bring Him to Hell like all other men, and keep Him there forever, the promise of Gen. 3:15 could never be fulfilled.

Satan attempted to kill Christ a number of times. We read about one attempt in Mat. 2.

Mat. 2:16 Then Herod, when he saw that he was mocked of the wise men, was exceeding wroth, and sent forth, and slew all the children that were in Bethlehem, and in all the coasts thereof, from two years old and under, according to the time which he had diligently enquired of the wise men.

Satan used Herod to try and destroy the child, Jesus Christ. But Satan's butchery did not find the child; he failed to kill the promised Seed.

Satan's final attempt to kill Christ was in crucifying Him.

It is here, on the cross, that Jesus[24] would confront Satan. The passage in Isaiah describes this confrontation.

Isa. 50: 6-8 I gave my back to the smiters, and my cheeks to them that plucked off the hair: I hid not my face from shame and spitting.
For the Lord GOD will help me; therefore shall I not be confounded: therefore have I set my face like a flint, and I know that I shall not be ashamed.
He is near that justifieth me; who will contend with me? let us stand together: who is mine adversary? let him come near to me.

---

[24] For such a monumental event one would think that Jesus would have shown up in all His power and glory. That the Seed would have come prepared to fight Satan. Much like a prized fighter going into the ring, that He would have been well nourished, strong, and ready for the battle. This was finally the moment. But we see Jesus Christ entering this most important of all conflicts weak and silent. He has no weapons, He calls for no angelic help, and He does no miracles. Instead He allows himself to be taken captive by the Roman guards. He willingly suffers their humiliation and mocking. They spit and buffet Him on the face. He is ridiculed and humiliated as He is whipped and beaten. A crown of thorns is planted on His head as He is paraded as a common criminal through the streets of Jerusalem. With His back torn open and bloodied and His face beaten to the point that no one could recognize Him, the Romans crucify Him. Crucifixion was a cruel way to die; it is a most tortuous and insidious way to put someone to death. Jesus Christ had His hands and feet nailed to a wooden cross and was left to struggle to breath. With every nerve ending screaming with pain and with every breath harder and harder to come by, Jesus Christ was now ready to confront Satan. One would look at the sight and think this is no way for the "Seed", Saviour of mankind to take on Satan. How could Satan be defeated by such a sight as this, our Hope, our Saviour nailed to a cross, bloodied beyond comprehension?

Jesus Christ willingly gave His face to "shame and spitting". He gave His "back to the smiters", and yet He had set His face "like a flint". He knew what He had to do and nothing was going to stop Him, not even the pain and shame of crucifixion.

Heb. 12:2b who for the joy that was set before him endured the cross, despising the shame,

It is here, at Calvary that He called for His "adversary", Satan.

Isa. 50: 8 He is near that justifieth me; who will contend with me? let us stand together: who is mine adversary? let him come near to me.

Jesus Christ, hanging from the cross, calls for Satan to come to Him. "Let us stand together", He called. "Come near to me", He was beckoning and challenging Satan when He said, "Who is my adversary?" In essence Jesus Christ was saying, "Come now Satan, here I am, come and get me. Now is your chance." Satan, witnessing the death of Jesus Christ, comes to the cross.

Satan approached Jesus Christ as He hung on the cross knowing that he would soon have Christ in Hell. Satan came to prosecute Christ, commit His soul to Hell, and have Him placed under the wrath of God just as he had done with all men before Him.

With the arrival of Satan, the courtroom of heaven is moved to the cross. God the Father is the Judge, Jesus Christ is the defendant, and Satan is the prosecutor. All the elements for a proper trial were in place.

God the Father, Who is witnessing this, does not come to the aid of His Son nor does He stop Satan from afflicting His Son. What God does, is lay all the sins of mankind on His Son.

2 Cor. 5:21 For he hath made him to be sin for us, who knew no sin; that we might be made the righteousness of God in him.

Jesus Christ is made sin; all the sins of the world are laid on him.

It is at this moment that darkness came.

Mar. 15:33 And when the sixth hour was come, there was darkness over the whole land until the ninth hour.[25]

It was during this darkness that Satan came to Jesus Christ to prosecute Him.

Satan is the chief prosecutor against those who sin. Satan prosecuted Jesus Christ of sin before the Father. He believed that if he could convict Jesus Christ of sin, He would be placed under the wrath of God like all men before Him. Satan believed that if he had a successful prosecution at the cross, he would win. Jesus Christ would be his prisoner in Hell; a place of no escape, no

---

[25] The darkness was not limited to the physical world. There was also the darkness of the spiritual world that arrived amassed.
Luk 22:53When I was daily with you in the temple, ye stretched forth no hands against me: but this is your hour, and the power of darkness.
The power of the darkness is Satan and all his host of evil beings; they came in power at this hour.

hope, and the promise of Gen. 3: 15 would forever be voided. Satan would have overcome the Seed; he would reign forever. To make sure everything went well, Satan called in his best legal team to help prove the charges against Jesus Christ.

Psalms 22 records the thoughts of Christ while on Calvary's cross.

Psa. 22:11 Be not far from me; for trouble is near; for there is none to help.

Satan has approached and is standing before Him now, "trouble is near". There is "none to help"; Christ is left alone to face Satan.

Psa. 22: 12-21 Many bulls have compassed me: strong bulls of Bashan have beset me round.
They gaped upon me with their mouths, as a ravening and a roaring lion.
I am poured out like water, and all my bones are out of joint: my heart is like wax; it is melted in the midst of my bowels.
My strength is dried up like a potsherd; and my tongue cleaveth to my jaws; and thou hast brought me into the dust of death.
For dogs have compassed me: the assembly of the wicked have inclosed me: they pierced my hands and my feet.
I may tell all my bones: they look and stare upon me.
They part my garments among them, and cast lots upon my vesture.
But be not thou far from me, O LORD: O my strength, haste thee to help me.

Deliver my soul from the sword; my darling from the power of the dog.
Save me from the lion's mouth: for thou hast heard me from the horns of the unicorns.

Christ, with His "bones out of joint", and His hands and feet "pierced" looked and saw the "lion", Satan.

The lion approached and with his "mouth" sought to devour Christ.

Christ saw Satan and also saw the "strong bulls of Bashan". There are many and they gathered around Him. Satan brought help, the "bulls of Bashan" to the cross. These "bulls" also "gaped" upon Jesus Christ with their "mouths".

Who are these "bulls of Bashan" that come with Satan to gape upon Jesus with their mouths? As in most prosecuting cases, there is often more than one lawyer who prosecutes the case. With this being the most important trial of the universe for Satan, he brings other lawyers, the best he has - the "bulls of Bashan". These "bulls" are devilish beings that come to assist Satan with the prosecution of Jesus. These "bulls" come from Bashan.[26]

---

[26]The scriptures refer to Bashan as the place where the best exists.
Duet. 32:14 Butter of kine, and milk of sheep, with fat of lambs, and rams of the breed of Bashan, and goats, with the fat of kidneys of wheat; and thou didst drink the pure blood of the grape.
Isa. 2:13 And upon all the cedars of Lebanon, that are high and lifted up, and upon all the oaks of Bashan,
God compares His hill to that of Bashan.

The scriptures state that Satan and his "bulls" "gaped upon" Jesus with their "mouths". But what does it mean to gape upon with their "mouths"? What were they doing to Christ?

Job tells us what this means.

Three men talked with Job while Satan persecuted him. These men did not comfort Job but accused him. They blamed Job for his suffering, they said he was a wicked man and therefore he deserved this punishment. They attacked Job and accused him of many sins, attempting to convict him and show that his suffering was deserved because he was an evil person. In one of Job's responses he made a statement similar to that made by Christ.

**Job 16: 1-11 Then Job answered and said,
I have heard many such things: miserable comforters are ye all.
Shall vain words have an end? or what emboldeneth thee that thou answerest?**

Ps. 68:15 The hill of God is as the hill of Bashan; an high hill as the hill of Bashan.
We see Amos prophecy against these evil "kine" or bulls of Bashon. God will one day deal with these bulls.
**Amo. 4:1-2 Hear this word, ye kine of Bashan, that are in the mountain of Samaria, which oppress the poor, which crush the needy, which say to their masters, Bring, and let us drink.
The Lord GOD hath sworn by his holiness, that, lo, the days shall come upon you, that he will take you away with hooks, and your posterity with fishhooks.**
It is also interesting to note that the giant,King Og, was from Bashan. He came out against Moses, Duet. 29:7.

I also could speak as ye do: if your soul were in my soul's stead, I could heap up words against you, and shake mine head at you.

But I would strengthen you with my mouth, and the moving of my lips should asswage your grief.

Though I speak, my grief is not asswaged: and though I forbear, what am I eased?

But now he hath made me weary: thou hast made desolate all my company.

And thou hast filled me with wrinkles, which is a witness against me: and my leanness rising up in me beareth witness to my face.

He teareth me in his wrath, who hateth me: he gnasheth upon me with his teeth; mine enemy sharpeneth his eyes upon me.

They have gaped upon me with their mouth; they have smitten me upon the cheek reproachfully; they have gathered themselves together against me.

God hath delivered me to the ungodly, and turned me over into the hands of the wicked.

Job looked out and he knew "ungodly" and "wicked" men surrounded him.

Job says that these three men have heaped up "words" against him. These "words" were condemning words; words that sought to convict Job as being guilty and deserving of the punishment he was experiencing. They accused him of many evils and sins. They sought to prove that Job was an unjust man. They accused Job of being a hypocrite and one who was not good and righteous. They condemned Job as being terrible and wicked.

Job says these "words" "teareth me". It was through these "words" that Job was "gnashed upon". He says "they have gaped upon me with their mouth". Job is referring to the "words" of condemnation that were spoken against him. These men prosecuted Job of sin.

From this passage we can now see what Jesus Christ was referring to when He used the same language in Psalm 22.

Psa. 22: 12-13 Many bulls have compassed me: strong bulls of Bashan have beset me round.
They gaped upon me with their mouths, as a ravening and a roaring lion.

Psa. 22: 21a Save me from the lion's mouth:

As Christ hung on the cross, Satan and his fellow henchmen verbally attacked Him. Satan "gaped upon" Jesus Christ with words, words of condemnation. Satan condemned Jesus Christ, convicting Him of sin.

Satan and his team of lawyers leveled charge after charge against Christ. All sin was charged to Him. There was not one sin that Satan didn't take the opportunity to accuse Christ with. Satan took great pleasure in condemning Christ, as this was his finest hour. He was displaying to God, and all of creation, that the promised Redeemer was being justly condemned.

Jesus speaks about this persecution in Psalms 71.

Psa. 71:10-11 For mine enemies speak against me; and they that lay wait for my soul take counsel together, Saying, God hath forsaken him: persecute and take him; for there is none to deliver him.

The "enemies" are Satan and his lawyers and they are after the "soul" of Christ. Satan took "counsel" with the bulls of Bashan to accomplish this. Satan says "God hath forsaken him: persecute and take him; for there is none to deliver him".

Jesus was guilty of every accusation made against Him. He had indeed become sin.

Peter writes that Christ bore our sins.

1 Pet. 2:24 Who his own self bare our sins in his own body on the tree,

The Psalmist writes concerning God the Son in Psa. 40.

Psa. 40: 12 For innumerable evils have compassed me about: mine iniquities have taken hold upon me, so that I am not able to look up; they are more than the hairs of mine head: therefore my heart faileth me.

The sins that God placed on His Son became His sins, "mine iniquities". The sins "take hold" of Jesus and they are "more than the hairs" of His head. Christ was identified with every sin and sinner. **This is how Satan was able to successfully prosecute Christ, because the Father had laid all the sins of mankind on His Son.**

Christ did not answer His accusers, neither Pilate nor Satan.

Isa. 53:7 He was oppressed, and he was afflicted, yet he opened not his mouth: he is brought as a lamb to the slaughter, and as a sheep before her shearers is dumb, so he openeth not his mouth.

At the end of three hours, which was the ninth hour, the darkness passed.

Mar. 15:33b there was darkness over the whole land until the ninth hour.

It was during these three hours of darkness that Satan presented all the evidence against Christ to the Father. Satan had successfully prosecuted Jesus Christ of sin and rested his case.

God the Father, who is the Judge, had the ultimate authority in this trial. He agreed with the evidence that Christ was made sin. The Father declared a verdict; Christ is guilty as charged. It is now; after the three hours of darkness, that God the Father forsook His Son.

Mar. 15:34 And at the ninth hour Jesus cried with a loud voice, saying, Eloi, Eloi, lama sabachthani? which is, being interpreted, My God, my God, why hast thou forsaken me?

Because Jesus was found to be guilty, the Father forsook Him, and now after the ninth hour, begins to pour out His wrath upon His Son. Christ, condemned, will now go to the torment side of Hell, forsaken of God.

CHAPTER 8

JESUS CHRIST IS CAST INTO HELL

We have seen how Satan prosecuted Christ at the cross. How Satan and his team of lawyers leveled every charge against Him. Christ hung on the cross with no answer, no response, no defense, for He was guilty. He is condemned of sin, guilty of every sin. Satan proved his case. With the trial at the cross over, Christ says "It is finished".

Jhn. 19:30 When Jesus therefore had received the vinegar, he said, It is finished: and he bowed his head, and gave up the ghost.

Christ said, "It is finished". The work of the cross was accomplished, but in addition we have learned that Christ is also referring to the completion of the trial that had just taken place. The prosecutors have ended their case against Him. The Judge, God the Father, found Him guilty. The trial is over; He will now be cast into Hell fire to suffer for all the sins that were placed on Him. With this He "gives up the ghost" and dies.

His soul left His body and started the journey toward Hell. His soul left Calvary, guilty, condemned, and forsaken of God; to suffer the torment of Hell, the just reward for a guilty condemned man.[27]

---

[27] Some teach and believe that the Lord went immediately to Abraham's bosom/ paradise because of His promise to the thief on the cross. "Today thou shalt be with me in paradise", however, before Christ could go to Paradise; He had to suffer the wrath of God in the torment side of Hell.

Psa. 42:5-7 Why art thou cast down, O my soul? and why art thou disquieted in me? hope thou in God: for I shall yet praise him for the help of his countenance.
O my God, my soul is cast down within me: therefore will I remember thee from the land of Jordan, and of the Hermonites, from the hill Mizar.
Deep calleth unto deep at the noise of thy waterspouts: all thy waves and thy billows are gone over me.

This passage speaks about the Lord's soul going to Hell. It was "cast down". No angels carried Him; He was forsaken of God and all alone. His soul entered the "waters"; the "waves" overtook Him as they crashed over Him.

Psa. 69:1-2 Save me, O God; for the waters are come in unto my soul.
I sink in deep mire, where there is no standing: I am come into deep waters, where the floods overflow me.

The waters came "unto" His "soul". He is drowned in the waters; there was no escape. He began to sink into the "deep mire". There was nothing to stand upon; there was "no standing".

Psa. 69:15 Let not the waterflood overflow me, neither let the deep swallow me up, and let not the pit shut her mouth upon me.

As Christ came through the deep mire, the "mouth" of Hell opened for Him. He saw "the pit" ready to receive Him. He is thrown into the torment side of Hell.

Psa. 88:4 I am counted with them that go down into the pit: I am as a man that hath no strength:

Because Jesus was numbered with the transgressors in life, He was numbered with those in "the pit".[28] He had "no strength". He suffered as those around Him suffered.

Psa. 88:6 Thou hast laid me in the lowest pit, in darkness, in the deeps.

He was cast to the "lowest pit", in "darkness".

He experienced "sorrows" and "pains" in Hell. He found "trouble".

Psa. 116:3 The sorrows of death compassed me, and the pains of hell gat hold upon me: I found trouble and sorrow.

This "trouble" is not the same "trouble" that He spoke of when being condemned of Satan on the cross in Psa.22:11. This "trouble" referred to Him experiencing God's wrath.

Christ was experiencing the "sorrows", "pains", and "trouble" because He was drinking from the cup of God's wrath.

Mat. 26:39 And he went a little further, and fell on his face, and prayed, saying, O my Father, if it be

---

[28] In all probability, as each soul enters Hell they are given a number, they are "counted". This way each soul can be accounted for and registered. We do the same in our prisons.

possible, let this cup pass from me: nevertheless not as I will, but as thou wilt.

We will talk more about this cup in the next chapter.

Christ prayed to the Father as He suffered the Father's wrath in the torment side of Hell.

Psa. 40: 17 But I am poor and needy; yet the Lord thinketh upon me: thou art my help and my deliverer; make no tarrying, O my God.

Even though God the Father had forsaken Him, Christ knew it would be the Father that would deliver Him. Christ trusted God to not leave His soul in Hell.

Act. 2: 27 Because thou wilt not leave my soul in hell, neither wilt thou suffer thine Holy One to see corruption.

Christ trusted the Father to bring Him out of prison.

Psa. 142:7 Bring my soul out of prison, that I may praise thy name: the righteous shall compass me about; for thou shalt deal bountifully with me.

Christ had complete faith in God, even as He suffered under the wrath of God. His faith was perfect, never wavering.

CHAPTER 9

THE PAYMENT HAS BEEN PAID

Satan thought he had won the battle. He was successful in having Christ be rejected of the Jews, crucified by Romans, and convicted of sin by God. Christ was now his prisoner in Hell suffering the wrath of God for sin. Satan was very pleased with himself, he rejoiced in this. He thought he had shown God to be a liar in that he triumphed over the promised Seed of the woman.

Throughout man's history, Satan had been able to accuse and hold all men in Hell. There never was a man who could pay the penalty for their sin and be released from Hell. All souls were justly being held in Hell. There was no payment that could be applied to the accused accounts to let them go free. Man's blood was never able to be a sufficient sacrifice, to make payment for sin. The blood of men was weak and without strength.

Satan thought the same would be true of Jesus Christ. But he miscalculated and misjudged the promised Seed. There was one thing that Satan overlooked, the blood of Christ.

Christ's body was special and unique and the blood of this body was God's blood.

Act. 20:28b the church of God, which he hath purchased with his own blood.

It was similar to man's blood in that it was red and flowed, but His blood was more than that. Christ's blood was able to accomplish something that no other man's blood was able to, and that was to make a perfect payment for sin.

When Christ became sin, Satan prosecuted Him. Satan charged Christ with every offence; each and every violation of the law was leveled against Him.[29] Satan did not leave one sin unaccounted for. Christ was declared guilty of the whole law by the Father and deserving of punishment.

Christ's soul was made an offering for sin.

Isa. 53:10 Yet it pleased the LORD to bruise him; he hath put him to grief: when thou shalt make his soul an offering for sin, he shall see his seed, he shall prolong his days, and the pleasure of the LORD shall prosper in his hand.

In becoming an offering for sin, Christ had to become sin and be killed. This was accomplished at the cross.

According to the law, after a sacrifice was killed it needed to be burned with fire. A sacrifice was not complete without fire. The fire would consume the sacrifice and cause it to become a sweet smelling savour. The offering was only made complete by fire.

---

[29] God took Satan in his own craftiness. In Satan's obsession to attack Christ with the law, he did the very thing that God wanted him to do, which was to prove that Christ was made to be sin. No one could ever say that Christ did not die for all sin, because Satan proved it in a court of law.

Lev. 1:9b and the priest shall burn all on the altar, to be a burnt sacrifice, an offering made by fire, of a sweet savour unto the LORD.

Lev. 1:13b and the priest shall bring it all, and burn it upon the altar: it is a burnt sacrifice, an offering made by fire, of a sweet savour unto the LORD.

The fire in the above verses represents the wrath of God being poured out on the offering. The same was true of Christ. Christ had to suffer the wrath of God being poured out on Him.

Mat. 26:42 He went away again the second time, and prayed, saying, O my Father, if this cup may not pass away from me, except I drink it, thy will be done.

Jesus Christ knew there was a "cup" He had to drink from. The contents of this cup represented the fire or wrath of God.

Rev. 14:10a The same shall drink of the wine of the wrath of God, which is poured out without mixture into the cup of his indignation;

The "wine of the wrath of God" was contained in this "cup". This "cup" is called the "cup of his indignation". Christ knew how terrible this "cup" was.

Luk. 22:42 Saying, Father, if thou be willing, remove this cup from me: nevertheless not my will, but thine, be done.

Luk. 22:44 And being in an agony he prayed more earnestly: and his sweat was as it were great drops of blood falling down to the ground.

He understood that this "cup" contained the "wrath of God". As He prayed, He began to "sweat as it were great drops of blood". This was all due to the "wrath" contained in this cup.[30]

After Christ was declared guilty and killed, He drank from the "cup of his indignation". He drank from this "cup" as He suffered in the torment side of Hell.

The fire/wrath of God caused Christ to become a "sweetsmelling savour".

Eph. 5:2 And walk in love, as Christ also hath loved us, and hath given himself for us an offering and a sacrifice to God for a sweetsmelling savour.

The law not only demanded fire, but it also required that the blood of the sin sacrifice be sprinkled on the altar.

Lev. 9:12 And he slew the burnt offering; and Aaron's sons presented unto him the blood, which he sprinkled round about upon the altar.

It was the blood that was to provide the payment for sins; the blood was shed and sprinkled at the altar to make this payment. The wrath of God would be removed after the blood made the payment. The problem was that throughout man's history there was never any blood that

---

[30] Unsaved man should also be sweating drops of blood at the prospect of drinking from this cup.

truly made a satisfactory payment for sins.

Heb. 10:4 For it is not possible that the blood of bulls and of goats should take away sins.

None of the sacrifices that were made could take away sin, for the blood that was sprinkled did not have the strength to remove sin. Even man's blood was useless. But this was not the case with Christ.

Heb. 12:24 And to Jesus the mediator of the new covenant, and to the blood of sprinkling, that speaketh better things than that of Abel.

Man's blood, as represented by Abel, had no strength to provide a payment for sin. But the blood of Christ had strength; it was "better" than man's. This is what Satan did not realize, that Christ had God's blood and that this blood had strength.

Christ's blood was sprinkled, "the blood of sprinkling", just as the law demanded.

Heb. 9:14a How much more shall the blood of Christ, who through the eternal Spirit offered himself without spot to God,

As Christ suffered in Hell, it was the Holy Spirit that offered the "blood of Christ" to God the Father.

Rom. 3:25a Whom God hath set forth to be a propitiation through faith in his blood,

His blood was able to do something that no other blood had been capable of doing. The blood of Christ had the strength to pay for sin and provide a satisfactory payment, a propitiation for sin. The blood of Christ satisfied the penalty that the law demanded and also satisfied the justice and holiness of God.

Col. 2: 14 Blotting out the handwriting of ordinances that was against us, which was contrary to us, and took it out of the way, nailing it to his cross;

The "blood of Christ" had the power to blot out the law. When Satan came to the cross to accuse Jesus Christ with sin, he brought the law with him. The law was nailed to the cross. The whole law was nailed to the cross; He was guilty of all of it. With the law nailed to the cross, the blood of Christ began to flow over the law. In fact, the verse states that the blood blotted out the law. The law could not be seen anymore as the blood of Christ covered, coated, and soaked the law; every part, jot, and tittle of it.

If there was a sin that was not paid for, Satan could have charged Jesus Christ with it at a later time. But they were all paid for. With the law blotted out by the blood of Christ, Satan is now powerless to accuse and prosecute because he has nothing more to charge the Lord Jesus Christ with.[31]

---

[31] If Satan would have known all that God could do through the blood of Christ he would never of crucified Him.
1 Cor. 2:8 Which none of the princes of this world knew: for had they known it, they would not have crucified the Lord of glory.
This is an important reason as to why God kept the mystery a secret until after Calvary when He revealed it to the Apostle Paul.
Eph. 3:3-4 How that by revelation he made known unto me the mystery; (as I wrote afore in few words,
Whereby, when ye read, ye may understand my knowledge in the mystery of Christ)

Heb. 12:24 And to Jesus the mediator of the new covenant, and to the blood of sprinkling, that speaketh better things than that of Abel.

The blood of Jesus Christ was shed on the cross. When Christ went to Hell, He was not held captive like other men. The blood of Christ has power, strength, and life. It has power to overcome death, strength to resurrect from the grave, and is able to grant life to those who trust in it. The blood of Christ is better than man's blood because it is God's blood.

What the blood of men could not do, the blood of Christ was able to perform. Men could not overcome sin, death, and the power of the Devil; but Christ does all these. He paid the penalty for sin, He defeated the enemy of death, and He conquered the Devil. Only through the blood of Christ do you find these victories and eternal life.

The blood of Christ speaks. It testifies to many wonderful blessings that flow from God to man. Let us listen to the scriptures as they reveal to us what the blood of Christ speaks.[32]

The blood of Christ speaks of peace with God.

Col. 1:20 And, having made peace through the blood of his cross, by him to reconcile all things unto himself; by him, I say, whether they be things in earth, or things in heaven.

---

[32] See the author's book, "The Way of Cain – The Creation of Man's Religion"

The blood of Christ speaks of justification.

Rom. 5:9 Much more then, being now justified by his blood, we shall be saved from wrath through him.

The blood of Christ speaks of redemption and the forgiveness of sins.

Eph. 1:7 In whom we have redemption through his blood, the forgiveness of sins, according to the riches of his grace;

The blood of Christ brings us near to God.

Eph. 2:13 But now in Christ Jesus ye who sometimes were far off are made nigh by the blood of Christ.

Our salvation is possible because of the blood of Jesus Christ. Only the blood of Jesus Christ has the power to pay for sin and to give forgiveness to mankind.

God offers man the blessings of what the blood of Christ speaks as a free gift, to be accepted by faith alone, without works. He only asks that you trust in the blood of Jesus Christ, that you cease from your works and lay hold of this most precious gift of God. Trust in the blood of Christ through faith. This is what the blood of Christ is speaking to you.

Rom. 3:25 Whom God hath set forth to be a propitiation through faith in his blood, to declare his righteousness for the remission of sins that are past, through the forbearance of God;

Rom. 3:28 Therefore we conclude that a man is

justified by faith without the deeds of the law.

Rom. 4:5 But to him that worketh not, but believeth on him that justifieth the ungodly, his faith is counted for righteousness.

Let us have faith in His blood and not in our own. We preach the blood of Christ and what it speaks—forgiveness of sins, victory over death, and eternal life.

CHAPTER 10

CHRIST DEPARTS FROM HELL

With the sin debt now paid by the blood of Christ, God's blood, Satan's accusations could no longer imprison the God-Man in Hell.

Act. 2:24 Whom God hath raised up, having loosed the pains of death: because it was not possible that he should be holden of it.

God the Father removes the "cup of his indignation" and "loosed the pains of death". It was "not possible" for Satan to hold Christ in Hell anymore, because the debt was paid.

Christ was free to leave. Satan could not stop Him.

Christ began His journey from the lowest Hell to Abraham's bosom/Paradise.

Christ moved upward from the torment side of Hell and toward the great gulf that divides Hell. No man had ever had the strength to cross the gulf, but now Christ crosses the gulf. In crossing the gulf separating the torment side from Abraham's bosom, He arrived in Paradise, just as He promised the thief on the cross.

Luk. 23:43 And Jesus said unto him, Verily I say unto thee, To day shalt thou be with me in paradise.

We know that Christ did not spend more than a part of a day in the torment side because He told the thief on the cross, "To day shalt thou be with me in paradise". Christ spent the next two days in Abraham's bosom fulfilling His words from Mat. 12:40.

Mat. 12:40 For as Jonas was three days and three nights in the whale's belly; so shall the Son of man be three days and three nights in the heart of the earth.

The souls in Paradise rejoiced in seeing the Son of God coming for them. After two days in Paradise, Christ opened Hell's mouth and led them out of prison. Isaiah and Psalms describe this.

Isa. 42:7 To open the blind eyes, to bring out the prisoners from the prison, and them that sit in darkness out of the prison house.

Isa. 61:1 The Spirit of the Lord GOD is upon me; because the LORD hath anointed me to preach good tidings unto the meek; he hath sent me to bind up the brokenhearted, to proclaim liberty to the captives, and the opening of the prison to them that are bound;

Psa. 146: 7b The LORD looseth the prisoners:

Christ says to the "prisoners" in Abraham's bosom, "Go forth".

Isa 49:9 That thou mayest say to the prisoners, Go forth; to them that are in darkness, Shew yourselves. They shall feed in the ways, and their pastures shall be in all high places.

These are truly great, wonderful and powerful words for Him to speak, "Go forth". All the saints from Abel, Noah, Abraham, David, and Daniel rejoiced to see this day and hear these words.

With the law nullified, Satan has lost his power to hold men in Hell; for, God could declare them righteous, based on His Son. Satan's accusations are now baseless for the price had been paid. God can say, "Go forth!"

The scriptures describe the path that Christ took when leaving Hell.

Psa. 40:2 He brought me up also out of an horrible pit, out of the miry clay, and set my feet upon a rock, and established my goings.

Christ came up out of the "horrible pit" and "out" of the "miry clay". His feet were set upon "a rock" outside of Hell.

When Christ victoriously left Hell, He took the keys of Hell with Him.

Rev. 1:18 I am he that liveth, and was dead; and, behold, I am alive for evermore, Amen; and have the keys of hell and of death.

The keys of Hell permitted Him to ascend out of "the pit".

Eph. 4:8 Wherefore he saith, When he ascended up on high, he led captivity captive, and gave gifts unto men (Now that he ascended, what is it but that he also descended first into the lower parts of the earth? He

that descended is the same also that ascended up far above all heavens, that he might fill all things.)

Christ "descended" "into the lower parts of the earth", Hell. He also "ascended" out of the lower parts and into the "heavens" themselves. As Christ left Hell, He "led captivity captive"; He took hold of Paradise. He held it captive; it was now His. Christ takes Paradise and its occupants, the righteous, to heaven.

For four thousand years of man's history, Hell was divided into two sections. Men went to one side or the other. Now that the blood of Christ paid the price of sin, the righteous were now released from Satan's grip and went with Christ to heaven. Christ brought Paradise and its saints to heaven, leaving the torment side in Hell.

2 Cor. 12:2 I knew a man in Christ above fourteen years ago, (whether in the body, I cannot tell; or whether out of the body, I cannot tell: God knoweth;) such an one caught up to the third heaven.

2 Cor. 12:4 How that he was caught up into paradise, and heard unspeakable words, which it is not lawful for a man to utter.

Paul tells us that Paradise is now in the third heaven where God resides.

Christ had the victory over death, Hell, and Satan. It is in Him we trust for these victories. Trust in the blood of Christ for the remission of sins and all of these victories will be yours in Christ.

THE ORDER OF THE EVENTS OF THE CROSS TILL THE RESURRECTION

A. Christ is born the Seed of the woman.

B. Satan has Christ crucified.

C. Christ is made sin by the Father.

D. Christ calls for Satan from the cross.

E. There is darkness at the sixth hour.

F. Satan approaches with his legal team and the trial starts.

G. Satan prosecutes Christ of sin.

H. The trial is over at the ninth hour as darkness leaves.

I. The Father declares Christ guilty.

J. The Father forsakes Christ.

K. Christ gives up the ghost.

L. Christ travels to Hell alone.

M. Christ arrives in the torment side of Hell.

N. Christ drinks from the cup of God's indignation.

O. The blood of Christ is sprinkled by the Holy Spirit.

P.   Christ is made a sweet smelling savour.

Q.   God the Father is satisfied with the payment.

R.   God the Father removes the cup of His indignation.

S.   Christ leaves the lower level of Hell and approaches the gulf.[33]

T.   Christ crosses the gulf and arrives in paradise during the first day.

U.   Christ spends the next two days in paradise.

V.   On the third day Christ opens the gates of Hell.

W.   Abraham's bosom is taken to the third heaven.

---

[33]We do not discuss this, but while Christ was in Hell, He preached to the spirits that are being held there, "prison".
1 Pet. 3:19 By which also he went and preached unto the spirits in prison;

CHAPTER 11

THE JUDGMENT OF THE UNRIGHTEOUS AND THE FINAL DESTINATION OF HELL

When Christ ascended out of Hell, He left the unrighteous souls in the torment side of it. This side of Hell continues to be filled with the souls of unrighteous men. These souls are awaiting God's judgment.

Heb. 9: 27 And as it is appointed unto men once to die, but after this the judgment:

God's judgment of all the unrighteous is described in Revelation.

Rev. 20: 11-15 And I saw a great white throne, and him that sat on it, from whose face the earth and the heaven fled away; and there was found no place for them.
And I saw the dead, small and great, stand before God; and the books were opened: and another book was opened, which is the book of life: and the dead were judged out of those things which were written in the books, according to their works.
And the sea gave up the dead which were in it; and death and hell delivered up the dead which were in them: and they were judged every man according to their works.
And death and hell were cast into the lake of fire. This is the second death.
And whosoever was not found written in the book of life was cast into the lake of fire.

The souls in Hell will be "delivered up" unto this judgment. Remember, Hell was created as a prison to house the souls of men until they are judged. This is the time that the unrighteous souls will be judged at the "great white throne". The occupants of Hell are now brought before God.

God has "books" at the "great white throne" judgment; they are the book of life, the book of the law, and the book of the works of men.

As each soul stands before God, a book will be opened in which their works have been recorded. Each and every work they did in life is recorded. Every time they blasphemed the name of God, every time they lied, every time they cheated, every time they disobeyed God, all is recorded in the book of works next to their name.

Mat. 12:36 But I say unto you, That every idle word that men shall speak, they shall give account thereof in the day of judgment.

The works recorded will be judged according to the book of the law.

The unrighteous souls at this judgment will be declared guilty because their works violated God's law. Paul describes this judgment in Rom. 2:16.

Rom. 2:16 In the day when God shall judge the secrets of men by Jesus Christ according to my gospel.

Paul, to whom it was given by the risen Christ, "to fulfill the word of God; Even the mystery" (Col.1:24b&25a) provides the basis for this judgment, which is his gospel.

The name of the accused will not be found in the book of life. God will pronounce judgment upon the guilty and the sentence will be immediately carried out. God will "cast" them into the "lake of fire"[34] to suffer for all of eternity.

Rev. 21: 8 But the fearful, and unbelieving, and the abominable, and murderers, and whoremongers, and sorcerers, and idolaters, and all liars, shall have their part in the lake which burneth with fire and brimstone: which is the second death.

All unrighteous men will be cast into the Lake of Fire and will burn and suffer forever and ever.[35] This is the judgment and penalty for those who are found guilty before God.

- The Final Destination of Hell -

---

[34] The Lake of Fire is not Hell. It is a separate place with a separate purpose. See the chapter on "The Lake of Fire".

[35] Christ became a sacrifice for sin at Calvary. Those who are cast into the Lake of Fire are souls who have rejected God's sacrifice. Unbelievers have chosen to be their own sacrifice, to pay for their sin themselves. God says that all sacrifices need to be salted, as stated in the law.

Lev. 2:13 And every oblation of thy meat offering shalt thou season with salt; neither shalt thou suffer the salt of the covenant of thy God to be lacking from thy meat offering: with all thine offerings thou shalt offer salt.

Eze43:24 And thou shalt offer them before the LORD, and the priests shall cast salt upon them, and they shall offer them up for a burnt offering unto the LORD.

Unrighteous souls will be salted with fire.

Mrk. 9:49 For every one shall be salted with fire, and every sacrifice shall be salted with salt.

Hell has been emptied as the souls have been presented before the Lord at the Great White Throne Judgment. God now casts Hell itself, into the Lake of Fire.

Rev. 20:14a And death and hell were cast into the lake of fire.

Now that Hell, the prison house, has fulfilled its purpose, God casts it into the "lake of fire". God no longer needs it. The Lake of Fire is the final destination of Hell.[36] The flames of Hell will forever burn in the Lake of Fire.

Mar. 9:45 And if thy foot offend thee, cut it off: it is better for thee to enter halt into life, than having two feet to be cast into hell, into the fire that never shall be quenched:

Jesus Christ said that the flames of Hell would never be "quenched" as they will continue to burn in the "lake of fire" forever.[37]

---

[36] It is probable that the structure of Hell is destroyed in the Lake of Fire. The bars, walls, sides, etc... may all burn up, as they are no longer needed. It is the flames of Hell that survive to burn forever.

[37] It is probable that the brimstone/fire God used when He created Hell came from the Lake of Fire.

CHAPTER 12

LAKE OF FIRE

God has prepared a place of eternal punishment for Satan and the angels that rebelled against Him. This place is called the Lake of Fire.

Mat. 25:41 Then shall he say also unto them on the left hand, Depart from me, ye cursed, into everlasting fire, prepared for the devil and his angels:

The Lake of Fire is not Hell; it is a separate and distinct place.[38] Many confuse the Lake of Fire and Hell, thinking they are one and the same. They are not. **Hell is a prison whose purpose is to hold the souls of men until they are brought before God at the Great White Throne Judgment. The Lake of Fire is a separate place whose purpose is to eternally punish those who are cast into it.**

The Lake of Fire was part of God's response to Satan's fall and rebellion. God prepared it to be the final destination for all those who revolted against His authority. Originally, only the Devil and his angels were to be cast there, but because man joined Satan in rebellion, he too now faces the Lake of Fire.

---

[38]Hell cannot be the Lake of Fire because in Rev. 20 we read that Hell is cast into the Lake of Fire.
Rev. 20:14 And death and hell were cast into the lake of fire. This is the second death.
Hell must be a separate place for it to be cast into the Lake of Fire.

The Lake of Fire burns with brimstone; this fire is "everlasting fire". It will burn for all of eternity.

The Devil will be cast into this lake.

Rev. 20: 10 And the devil that deceived them was cast into the lake of fire and brimstone, where the beast and the false prophet are, and shall be tormented day and night for ever and ever.

Those who are cast into this lake will be tormented "day and night" experiencing God's perfect justice forever. Everything God does is perfect, and this is no exception. The torment will never stop, but will constantly afflict those found there. This torment will last "for ever and ever". The scriptures are very clear; the torment is everlasting, forever and ever. There is no escape or release from this place.

The beast and the false prophet, both followers of Satan, will be cast into the Lake of Fire.

Rev. 19:20 And the beast was taken, and with him the false prophet that wrought miracles before him, with which he deceived them that had received the mark of the beast, and them that worshipped his image. These both were cast alive into a lake of fire burning with brimstone.

Those who receive the mark of the beast will also be cast into the Lake of Fire. Their sin, in taking this mark, seals their fate. They will be cast into the Lake of Fire at the Great White Throne Judgment.

Rev. 14: 9-11 And the third angel followed them, saying with a loud voice, If any man worship the beast and his image, and receive his mark in his forehead, or in his hand,

The same shall drink of the wine of the wrath of God, which is poured out without mixture into the cup of his indignation; and he shall be tormented with fire and brimstone in the presence of the holy angels, and in the presence of the Lamb:

And the smoke of their torment ascendeth up for ever and ever: and they have no rest day nor night, who worship the beast and his image, and whosoever receiveth the mark of his name.

Those in the Lake of Fire will drink from the "cup of his indignation"; this "cup" contains the "wine of the wrath of God". Having rejected God's grace and goodness, they will now drink from this "cup" eternally.

The "torment" of the souls in the Lake of Fire is in the presence of the "holy angels" and the "Lamb", the Lord Jesus Christ.

God is pleased, because His perfect righteousness and justice is finally being expressed in what He has done with those who have transgressed against Him, and He demonstrates this to all His creation, for all eternity.

The "smoke of their torment" will arise forever as a permanent testimony of God's perfect and holy justice.

There is "no rest" in the Lake of Fire. There are two meanings to this "rest". One meaning is that those who are in the Lake of Fire will be constantly working and laboring, never to cease, pause, or rest. The second meaning relates to God's "rest". God provides a "rest" to those who are His.

Heb. 4:9 There remaineth therefore a rest to the people of God.

Those who enter into God's "rest" cease from work.

Heb. 4:10 For he that is entered into his rest, he also hath ceased from his own works, as God did from his.

Man can cease from his "own works" and "rest" with God.

Those who are in the Lake of Fire will not enter into God's "rest"; they will never experience it. They will be "tormented with fire and brimstone" forever; they will have "no rest" forever and ever.

All unrighteous men will be judged at the Great White Throne Judgment. It is at this trial that men will be justly condemned. The punishment will be the Lake of Fire. The only way for man to avoid the Lake of Fire is to have his name written in the book of life. Anyone whose name is not written in the book of life will be cast into the Lake of Fire.

Rev. 20:15b And whosoever was not found written in the book of life was cast into the lake of fire.

The Apostle Paul provides more information about the Lake of Fire.

2 The. 1:8-9 In flaming fire taking vengeance on them that know not God, and that obey not the gospel of our Lord Jesus Christ:
Who shall be punished with everlasting destruction from the presence of the Lord, and from the glory of his power;

Those who do not "obey the gospel of our Lord Jesus Christ" will be "punished with everlasting destruction". The "everlasting destruction" will take place in the Lake of Fire. The destruction will never end because the "worm dieth not", Mar. 9:48.

This is why it is called "everlasting destruction".

The wrath of God will be ever present upon all the souls in the Lake of Fire.

Jhn. 3:36 He that believeth on the Son hath everlasting life: and he that believeth not the Son shall not see life; but the wrath of God abideth on him.

God's wrath abides forever on the unrighteous; it will never be removed.

The unrighteous have earned the wrath of God. In fact, they have treasured it up.

Rom. 2:5 But after thy hardness and impenitent heart treasurest up unto thyself wrath against the day of wrath and revelation of the righteous judgment of God;

Man has hardened his heart against God, and in so doing he has reserved unto himself wrath. This is what man's impenitent, unrepentant, hardened heart has earned, God's wrath. Man has accumulated, collected, and laid up wrath that will be paid to him in full at the "day of wrath".

The Lake of Fire is where God will pour out His wrath on the unrighteous for all of eternity. The fierceness of God will be visited on all those in the Lake of Fire. The almighty power of God will come thundering down as it inflicts the most terrible misery on the lost. God will not restrain or withdraw His fury as it is loosed upon the unrighteous. God's wrath will know no limits, His anger will not be lessoned, and His fury will not be lightened. There will be no pity shown, no compassion, no withdrawal of His cup from those who have transgressed against Him. The Lake of Fire is where God will manifest His wrath, which will burn forever those who are cast there. A perfect God will perfectly execute His judgment for all eternity in the Lake of Fire.

This is the judgment of an infinite God. The justice and holiness of God demand none less than eternal punishment. The unrighteous have transgressed a thrice-holy God; they have earned this eternal wrath thrice over. The unrighteous have "trodden under foot the Son of God".

Heb. 10:29 Of how much sorer punishment, suppose ye, shall he be thought worthy, who hath trodden under foot the Son of God, and hath counted the blood of the covenant, wherewith he was sanctified, an unholy thing, and hath done despite unto the Spirit of grace?

The "sorer punishment" for the souls who have "trodden under foot the Son of God" will be meted out by God for all of eternity in the Lake of Fire. **All those who are cast into the Lake of Fire are deserving of God's "sorer punishment" because they all have "trodden under foot the Son of God".**

God will view those in the Lake of Fire with contempt as He pours out His wrath.

Dan. 12:2 And many of them that sleep in the dust of the earth shall awake, some to everlasting life, and some to shame and everlasting contempt.

God will forever have contempt toward the unrighteous. Contempt means to hate with extreme hatred, to deem as worthless, vile, to disdain. Contempt is "one of the strongest expressions of a mean opinion which the English language affords".[39] This is God's attitude, thought, and opinion toward those in the Lake of Fire. He will hold them in contempt forever. He knows their wicked hearts and has no pity on them; there is no room for sorrow, compassion, or sadness. His attitude will not change. He will never be moved from this position; He will never stem the flow of His unbridled wrath.

Saints should agree with God and view these damned souls the same way that He does, with contempt. For saints to view them, other than how God does, is sin.

---

[39] American Dictionary of the English Language, Noah Webster, ninth edition 1997

CHAPTER 13

SATAN'S FINAL DESTINATION

Satan's attempt to defeat the "seed" at the cross had failed. Christ had the victory. But after Calvary, God allowed Satan to continue in his rebellion. The scriptures teach that there is a day in which God will cause Satan to fall and destroy him. Isaiah describes this fall of Satan.

Isa. 14: 4-6 That thou shalt take up this proverb against the king of Babylon, and say, How hath the oppressor ceased! the golden city ceased!
The LORD hath broken the staff of the wicked, and the sceptre of the rulers.
He who smote the people in wrath with a continual stroke, he that ruled the nations in anger, is persecuted, and none hindereth.

The king of Babylon in Isa. 14:4 is Lucifer in verse 12.

Isa. 14:12a O Lucifer, son of the morning!

This passage describes the fall of his kingdom and his own personal fall. It is Satan "who ruled the nations", for he is the "god of this world", 2 Cor. 4:4. Satan "ruled the nations in anger"; Satan is filled with fury, rage, and anger and this is how he ruled.[40]

---

[40] The world is filled with this anger. The world is not a loving, kind, merciful place; but instead it is mean, dictatorial, and hateful. The world is just like the god it has chosen to worship. Satan leaves no room for love, joy, or peace.

But Satan is now "persecuted". The prosecutor has now become the persecuted. God will destroy Satan; He will put an end to the tyranny of Satan's rule and kingdom. No one can stop God from fulfilling this verse; there is "none" that can "hindereth" God.

With the fall of Satan, the earth will sing.

Isa. 14:7 The whole earth is at rest, and is quiet: they break forth into singing.

The "whole earth" rejoices, every part of it. Satan used to be able to walk up and down in the earth but now he has been removed. This will truly be a joyful day.

Isa. 14: 9 Hell from beneath is moved for thee to meet thee at thy coming:

"Hell", yes it is Hell that Satan will be delivered to. Hell will now become Satan's prison. Before we discuss Satan's arrival in Hell we will look at how Satan will be captured.

Rev. 20: 1-3 And I saw an angel come down from heaven, having the key of the bottomless pit and a great chain in his hand.
And he laid hold on the dragon, that old serpent, which is the Devil, and Satan, and bound him a thousand years,
And cast him into the bottomless pit, and shut him up, and set a seal upon him, that he should deceive the nations no more, till the thousand years should be fulfilled: and after that he must be loosed a little season.

God allowed Satan freedom to roam after Calvary until the set time came to capture him. When the time comes, God will send an angel[41] to bind Satan.[42] God's angel will lay "hold" on Satan and bind him with a great chain. With Satan bound, God's angel will take him all the way to Hell. Satan will be paraded through Hell as he is being taken to the bottomless pit. Isaiah describes Satan's decent into Hell.

Isa. 14: 9-12 Hell from beneath is moved for thee to meet thee at thy coming: it stirreth up the dead for thee, even all the chief ones of the earth; it hath raised up from their thrones all the kings of the nations.
All they shall speak and say unto thee, Art thou also become weak as we? Art thou become like unto us?
Thy pomp is brought down to the grave, and the noise of thy viols: the worm is spread under thee, and the worms cover thee.
How art thou fallen from heaven, O Lucifer, son of the morning! How art thou cut down to the ground, which didst weaken the nations!

God shakes and "stirreth" up all the inhabitants of Hell. It is as if God were saying, "Get up and arise, for here comes your god, the one you all trusted in, look and behold him." God wants everyone in Hell to witness the defeat of Satan. All the "chief ones" arise; all the souls will watch Satan be dragged down into its depths.

---

[41] The name of this angel is not given here in the scriptures. But it very well could be Michael. He battled and overcame Satan earlier in the heavens. Rev. 12:7.
[42] There will probably be a great battle that takes place as Satan summons all of his devils to try and protect himself. But God's angel will overcome all the hordes of the Devil until he reaches Satan.

With Hell ready to receive its prisoner, God's angel enters with Satan bound in a great chain. The inhabitants start to shout and hiss at Satan as he passes by them. They mock him and torment him with their words. They shout, "art thou also become weak as we?" They are saying, "Look at you, you are no different then us now. We have no strength in this prison and now you are here with us. You, who claimed to be a god, are nothing now, you are weak and pathetic now."

As Satan is mocked, it is possible that some may call him Buddha, Ala, Ra, Diana, Aster, etc..., for Satan had many names as the "god of this world". The souls in Hell will know that the god they had trusted in, whatever the name, was not God.

They jeer and mock him as he makes his way down the descending passageway. They realize that their god is now "become like unto us". Satan will be truly like those incarcerated in Hell; he will be imprisoned, without strength, and suffering the torments.

Isaiah talks about the "noise of thy viols".[43] This noise is coming from Satan. He does not want to be incarcerated here.

The "worms" surround Satan, they cover him, mocking and hissing at him, as he is taken through their midst toward the bottomless pit. Once God's angel reaches the

---

[43] Viol refers to a musical instrument. Satan was created with wonderful pipes that could create beautiful sounds. But as he is dragged through Hell the wonderful melodies he used to create are now replaced with noise, the noise of his crying and screaming.

bottomless pit, he uses the key that he had in Rev. 20:1 and opens it.

Rev. 20:3a And cast him into the bottomless pit, and shut him up, and set a seal upon him,

With the door open to the bottomless pit, Satan is cast in and the door is shut. With Satan sealed in the pit, God's angel leaves; leaving all the unrighteous "worms" behind him in Hell.

Isa. 14:12 O Lucifer, son of the morning! How art thou cut down to the ground, which didst weaken the nations!

"O Lucifer", what an end. Locked away in the great furnace of the bottomless pit. The once proud adversary of God is now His prisoner in Hell.

Rev. 20:3b till the thousand years should be fulfilled: and after that he must be loosed a little season.

Satan will be tormented in the bottomless pit for a thousand years, after which he will be "loosed".

Rev. 20:7 And when the thousand years are expired, Satan shall be loosed out of his prison,

During Satan's stay in "his prison"/bottomless pit he will never repent of the evil that he caused. He will never turn to God for mercy. The flames of Hell fire will never cause him to become obedient to God. Satan will still be rebellious, even after his time in Hell.

We know this to be true, because after one thousand years he once again sets out to deceive the nations.

Rev. 20: 8-9 And shall go out to deceive the nations which are in the four quarters of the earth, Gog and Magog, to gather them together to battle: the number of whom is as the sand of the sea.
And they went up on the breadth of the earth, and compassed the camp of the saints about, and the beloved city: and fire came down from God out of heaven, and devoured them.

Satan gathers mankind in one last battle against God. God answers Satan's revolt with fire. God will send "fire" out of heaven, which will devour Satan and his followers.

After this battle, God will take Satan and cast him into the Lake of Fire.

Rev. 20:10 And the devil that deceived them was cast into the lake of fire and brimstone, where the beast and the false prophet are, and shall be tormented day and night for ever and ever.

The Lake of Fire that God prepared for Satan will be his end. Satan shall be "tormented" day and night. The torment shall never cease. Satan will be there "for ever and ever", for all of eternity. This is Satan's end for all of eternity.

God will fulfill His promise of Gen 3:15.

Gen. 3:15 And I will put enmity between thee and the woman, and between thy seed and her seed; it shall bruise thy head, and thou shalt bruise his heel.

CHAPTER 14

FOREVER UNREPENTANT

The scriptures state that those who are cast into the Lake of Fire will be there forever and ever. This means that they will never be removed, let out, or released. Those in the Lake of Fire will never be annihilated nor cease to exist; the worm cannot die. They will be experiencing the flames forever.

There are many people, saved and lost, who object to the thought of eternal punishment for the lost. They hear from preachers and believe that the torments of Hell or the Lake of Fire will cause these poor souls to be repentant and wishing they had received Jesus Christ as their Saviour while they were alive. But because they died in unbelief, they now will pay the price for all of eternity because God will not accept their repentant heart and be merciful, now that they have seen the light. This unscriptural understanding portrays the Lord as being unjust, unfair, unmerciful, and unloving. Those holding this position are really attacking God's righteousness, justice, and holiness as He perfectly executes His wrath on the lost forever.

The truth of the matter is that unrighteous men will never repent in Hell or the Lake of Fire. The flames of torment will not produce a repentant heart; they will not cause the lost souls to turn to God. Instead, as time goes by they will become angrier and angrier with God. They will blame Him for their torment. They will accuse God of being unjust in His condemnation of their works. They will blaspheme and damn God with each breath. The flames will not diminish either Satan's or man's rebellion; instead it will grow as they will continue to hate God for all of eternity.

There are a number of examples of torment not causing a change of heart in scripture.

The first example is Satan in the bottomless pit.

The torment and flames of the furnace of the bottomless pit will not cause Satan to repent, even after one thousand years of suffering the wrath of God. He will continue in his rebellion and hatred of God. The same is true of all the unrighteous souls.

The second example is the rich man.

The rich man in Luke 16 never repented, even though there are those who think that he did from reading the passage. He did not, but continued in his rebellion against God's authority. Lets read the passage.

Luk. 16:27-31 Then he said, I pray thee therefore, father, that thou wouldest send him to my father's house:
For I have five brethren; that he may testify unto them, lest they also come into this place of torment.
Abraham saith unto him, They have Moses and the prophets; let them hear them.
And he said, Nay, father Abraham: but if one went unto them from the dead, they will repent.
And he said unto him, If they hear not Moses and the prophets, neither will they be persuaded, though one rose from the dead.

Here the rich man is talking with Abraham. The rich man doesn't like his circumstances but that is different than repenting and seeking God's mercy and grace. We do not see the rich man repenting, he is not sorry for his sins, and he is not calling upon God for mercy.

The fact that the rich man does not want his brothers to come into the place of torment has nothing to do with him repenting. He just doesn't want to see them suffer. He speaks to Abraham about his brothers. Abraham responds, "They have Moses and the prophets; let them hear them." Abraham is saying that God has given warning and instructions, which are found in scriptures written by Moses and the prophets. This is all the warning that is needed to escape Hell. God spoke through those men and God expects men to listen to them.

The rich man does not say, "you are right, God has given salvation in the scriptures, my brothers can escape this torment if they would believe God as He spoke through Moses and the prophets." Instead, the rich man argues. He says "Nay". He thinks he knows better. He wants to tell God how to do things. This is rebellion against God's authority. The rich man has not repented and he has not placed himself under God's authority. He still wants to tell God what to do.

We also see the rich man ask for water, but we do not see him ask for forgiveness of sins, God's mercy, or God's grace.

Another example of the hardness of man's heart is seen during the tribulation.

In the book of Revelation we see God beginning to pour out His wrath on mankind during the tribulation.

Rev. 16:9 And men were scorched with great heat, and blasphemed the name of God, which hath power over these plagues: and they repented not to give him glory.

Rev. 16:11 And blasphemed the God of heaven because of their pains and their sores, and repented not of their deeds.

These men do not repent; they do not turn to God for help, mercy, and or grace. Instead, as God pours out more vials of wrath, they blaspheme God and their anger against God only increases. This is hard for us to understand because we would expect that when God pours out His wrath that men would seek God's mercy; but they do just the opposite, they blaspheme God. [44]

- No Hope -

The scriptures state that there is no hope; it does not exist, for those unrighteous men who have gone to Hell.

Isa. 38:18 For the grave cannot praise thee, death can not celebrate thee: they that go down into the pit cannot hope for thy truth.

---

[44]Perhaps one of the best examples of God's torment not bringing repentance is Pharaoh. Pharaoh knew that Moses' God was God and yet he continued to harden his heart with every plague brought upon him. He never repented. He would go to Hell that way and remain that way for all of eternity.

Isaiah states that those who are unrighteous and in "the pit" "cannot hope for thy truth". **The souls in Hell cannot change; they "cannot" hope for truth. The reason for this is because these souls will not.** The unrighteous dead will not repent, they will not obey God, and they will not change their hearts. They will never look to God for "hope", they will forever and ever resist God. Thus God says they "cannot hope for thy truth".

Their hearts are hardened against God. The flames of Hell and the Lake of Fire will not soften them. Instead, man will only harden his heart more and more against God.

1 The. 4:13 But I would not have you to be ignorant, brethren, concerning them which are asleep, that ye sorrow not, even as others which have no hope.

Paul writes that those who die in unrighteousness "have no hope". The unrighteous will always remain unrighteous; they will never repent nor submit to God. There is "no hope" for anyone who dies in their sins. The reason God says there is "no hope" is because the lost will continue in rebellion and unbelief for all of eternity.

God did not create Hell and the Lake of Fire to bring the damned to a state of repentance; He designed them as a place for punishment.

It's God's goodness, not His punishment, that brings repentance.

The scriptures tell us that it is God's goodness that brings repentance.

Rom. 2:4 Or despisest thou the riches of his goodness and forbearance and longsuffering; not knowing that the goodness of God leadeth thee to repentance?

God says that His "goodness leadeth" to "repentance"[45], not His wrath.

God's "goodness" is seen in the world we live in and it is not found in Hell or the Lake of Fire. Only now, while one is alive in this life, can one see the "goodness of God", repent, and find hope.

Ecc. 9:4 For to him that is joined to all the living there is hope:

Hope only exists in this life and cannot be found in Hell or the Lake of Fire.[46] Hope can only be found now, while one is alive.

The love of God is designed to cause repentance. The love of God is the most powerful motivator God can use to try and bring man into a state of repentance. If man rejects the love of God, then there is no hope. If man will not repent when experiencing God's love, he will never repent. **Eternal punishment will not achieve what God's love doesn't achieve. The fires of Hell and the Lake of Fire are not stronger and more productive in bringing men to repentance than God's love displayed through the death of Christ at Calvary.**

---

[45] Repentance is changing one's mind. In the scriptures, when one believes the gospel (places his faith in Christ), he has repented from trusting someone or something else.

[46] There is always "hope" for those who are alive. No matter how dire the circumstances or how depressing life may seem, there is "hope".

God has displayed His "goodness" to all men everywhere, without exception.

Psa. 98:2 The LORD hath made known his salvation: his righteousness hath he openly shewed in the sight of the heathen.

God's "salvation" has been made "known" and "openly shewed in the sight of the heathen." God's saving grace is seen by all men.

Tts. 2:11 For the grace of God that bringeth salvation hath appeared to all men,

There is no man who has not seen God's grace; it "hath appeared to all men". Every man, in every jungle, city, desert, mountain, or island, can see God's grace. God has shown His "goodness" to everyone, knowing that it can lead men to "repentance".[47]

No man will be able to accuse God and say they did not know of God's "goodness", "grace", "righteousness", or "salvation".

Rom. 1:20 For the invisible things of him from the creation of the world are clearly seen, being understood by the things that are made, even his eternal power and Godhead; so that they are without excuse:

---

[47]It is a tactic of the Devil when the skeptic questions, "How can a man be saved if he lives in the jungle and has never seen a Bible or heard the name of Jesus Christ?" This is a foolish and unlearned question. God's word makes known how His "grace...that bringeth salvation" reaches every man in every corner of the world.

There is no "excuse" for man; they all know of God's "goodness" that "leadeth" to "repentance", for God has shown it to all men.

God has made His "goodness" and "grace" known to all men because He wants all to be saved.

1 Tim. 2:4 Who will have all men to be saved, and to come unto the knowledge of the truth.

It is God's will that "all men" "be saved". God has done everything needed to save "all men".

God offers salvation as a free gift.

Rom. 5:18b even so by the righteousness of one the free gift came upon all men unto justification of life.

This "free gift" has come unto "all men". All have been offered this "free gift".

Eph. 2:8 For by grace are ye saved through faith; and that not of yourselves: it is the gift of God:

God only asks that man accept His free gift of salvation through faith. All men can believe and be saved.

Rom. 2:4a Or despisest thou the riches of his goodness and forbearance and longsuffering;

Unfortunately, many men reject God's "goodness"; they despise it. They willfully refuse to accept the "free gift"; they choose to rebel against God.

Jhn. 3:19-20 And this is the condemnation, that light is come into the world, and men loved darkness rather than light, because their deeds were evil.
For every one that doeth evil hateth the light, neither cometh to the light, lest his deeds should be reproved.

God's light has "lighted every man"[48]. But men, because their deeds are evil, love darkness rather than light. Jesus' own words, here in John 3, tell us why souls refuse the light. They hate it. And they will hate it forever.

Rom. 1:32 Who knowing the judgment of God, that they which commit such things are worthy of death, not only do the same, but have pleasure in them that do them.

Men choose "death" instead of life with God, darkness rather than light. Men choose to suffer the "judgment of God" rather than repent and accept His free gift. In fact, they take "pleasure" in rejecting God and sinning against Him. Of their own free will they reject God's "goodness" and with "pleasure" they mock, scoff, and hate God.

God will not force a man to believe, He will not violate man's free will. He allows men to choose their own eternal future. He has done everything needed to bring men to Himself through His "goodness" that is seen by all men.

No one in Hell or the Lake of Fire will ever repent, or cease from rebelling against God. They will continue for

---

[48] **Jhn. 1:9 That was the true Light, which lighteth every man that cometh into the world.**

all of eternity to hate God. They will not like the circumstances they find themselves in but they will never repent because of them. They will continue in their hatred of God.

Everything God does is perfect. His salvation of the saved is perfect and the execution of His wrath is also perfect.

Conclusion

God built a prison that is called Hell. Today, God is casting and holding the souls of unrighteous men in Hell to await their final judgment.

We have learned that it is God's goodness that leadeth man to faith and eternal life. Part of God's goodness is His revelation of the truths about Hell. God warns man of Hell and the torments found there. He does not wish any man to suffer in the flames of Hell or the Lake of Fire. He has done everything possible, with the exception of forcing man to believe, to provide salvation for all men to escape these terrible places.

Believers who know the truth about Hell and the judgment to come should warn the unrighteous just as the scriptures do. We who know of the torments and flames, the pain and sorrow, the wailing and moaning that will occur to those who die in unbelief need to proclaim God's great salvation.

1 Cor. 5:11a Knowing therefore the terror of the Lord, we persuade men;

We have learned of "the terror of the Lord" and seen how it will be executed on the unrighteous. The Apostle Paul warned those he witnessed to of this terror, the judgment to come. We should follow Paul's example as written in Acts.

Act. 24:25 And as he reasoned of righteousness, temperance, and judgment to come, Felix trembled,

and answered, Go thy way for this time; when I have a convenient season, I will call for thee.

Set forth Hell and the Lake of Fire before the unjust eyes. It is better for the unbeliever to see Hell now; per chance they repent, for if they die in unbelief they will definitely see it as they enter Hell's mouth.

Men should not mock or scoff at Hell or the judgment to come. Men should tremble, as Felix trembled[49], at the prospect of facing God's judgment. Tremble at the full fury of God's wrath being poured out, at the fierceness of God's anger being unleashed upon all those who have rejected Him. There will be no compassion from God, no pity, no mercy, no moderation. God will show only anger, fury, fire, and contempt to those who stand before Him in rebellion. Vengeance will be God's as He executes His infinite justice infinitely. For all of eternity, God will cause those in the Lake of Fire to drink from the cup of His indignation and wrath. He will never remove it, never weaken it, and never dilute it. Tremble now, and seek God. Yes, man should tremble at the thought of facing God at this judgment.

Those who are saved have the opportunity, responsibility, and privilege to seek the lost, the unrighteous, and unbelievers and display God's great love to them. Do not neglect or shrug from this endeavor. The eternities of souls are at stake. There is no greater work that can be taken upon your shoulders, no greater plow to lean into. This is why God gives the same occupation to all of those who are saved, that of an ambassador. As ambassadors for Christ we should use our time in this life

---

[49]His trembling should have resulted in him believing but it did not.

to convince, urge, and persuade the unsaved to accept God's free gift of salvation. We are to bring God's grace, peace, and life to those who face eternal wrath, fury, and death.

2 Cor. 6:2 (For he saith, I have heard thee in a time accepted, and in the day of salvation have I succoured thee: behold, now is the accepted time; behold, now is the day of salvation.)

Today is the day of salvation. No one knows what tomorrow may bring;

Prov. 27:1 Boast not thyself of to morrow; for thou knowest not what a day may bring forth.

No one is guaranteed another day, so let it be today that salvation is preached. Now is the time, not later. Do not waste the time; for, the time is short, the hour is nearer now for the judgment to come.

APPENDIX 1

THE GRAVE AND SLEEP

The word "grave" in the scriptures refers to a hole in the ground; a body is then placed in it.

Gen 50:5 My father made me swear, saying, Lo, I die: in my grave which I have digged for me in the land of Canaan, there shalt thou bury me. Now therefore let me go up, I pray thee, and bury my father, and I will come again.

Another word for grave is "tomb".

Job 21:32 Yet shall he be brought to the grave, and shall remain in the tomb.

A tomb was cut into the side of a hill or mountain; this became the grave.

The dead body or "carcase" was laid in the "grave".

1 Ki. 13:30 And he laid his carcase in his own grave; and they mourned over him, saying, Alas, my brother!

Many times, relatives wanted to be buried next to their deceased family members. They wanted all of their graves to be next to one another.

2 Sam. 19:37a Let thy servant, I pray thee, turn back again, that I may die in mine own city, and be buried by the grave of my father and of my mother.

Dead bodies that are in the grave are unable to do anything because the body is only an empty earthen vessel. The soul and the spirit, which gives it life, have departed.

Ecc. 9:10 Whatsoever thy hand findeth to do, do it with thy might; for there is no work, nor device, nor knowledge, nor wisdom, in the grave, whither thou goest.

Obviously, the dead vessel cannot work, have knowledge, or any understanding. It is completely useless without the spirit or soul.

The word "sleep" is often used in reference to the death of the body.

Jhn. 11:12-13a Then said his disciples, Lord, if he sleep, he shall do well.
Howbeit Jesus spake of his death:

Jesus used the word "sleep" when He spoke about the death of Lazarus. This is referring to the physical body only, the spirit and soul have left.

Job describes those who are dead as "sleep".

Job 14:12 So man lieth down, and riseth not: till the heavens be no more, they shall not awake, nor be raised out of their sleep.

Job is talking about their physical bodies. These sleeping/dead bodies will become "awake" when they are given life again at the resurrection, when the spirit and soul re-enter the body.

Dan. 12:2 And many of them that sleep in the dust of the earth shall awake, some to everlasting life, and some to shame and everlasting contempt.

In the above verse we see those that "sleep" in the dust of the earth, this is describing the dead physical body. These bodies will be raised from the dust of the earth, some to everlasting life and some to everlasting contempt.

The scriptures never use the word "sleep" to indicate that those who die are in an unconscious state. As we have seen, the soul and spirit are fully aware at death, they are conscious. It is the body that sleeps.

2 Ki. 22:20 Behold therefore, I will gather thee unto thy fathers, and thou shalt be gathered into thy grave in peace; and thine eyes shall not see all the evil which I will bring upon this place. And they brought the king word again.

In the above verse a distinction is made between the physical body and the soul. When the verse states, "I will gather thee unto thy fathers" it is stating that the soul will be gathered to his family. The verse then states that the dead body will be "gathered into thy grave". The body goes to the "grave" and the soul goes to be with his fathers. The angels will "gather" the righteous soul while men will "gather" the body.

APPENDIX 2

JESUS' USE OF THE WORD HELL

When Jesus mentioned "Hell" in the four gospels, He was referring to the literal Hell found, "down", in the center of the earth.

Luk. 10:15 And thou, Capernaum, which art exalted to heaven, shalt be thrust down to hell.

Mat. 11:23 And thou, Capernaum, which art exalted unto heaven, shalt be brought down to hell:

Jesus talked about the gates of Hell. These gates would not be able to prevail against Him.

Mat. 16:18 And I say also unto thee, That thou art Peter, and upon this rock I will build my church; and the gates of hell shall not prevail against it.

The gates of Hell did not keep Christ imprisoned. They could not "prevail" against Him, as He had the keys and power to open them.

Jesus said Hell was filled with fire.

Mar. 9:47 And if thine eye offend thee, pluck it out: it is better for thee to enter into the kingdom of God with one eye, than having two eyes to be cast into hell fire:

Mat. 18:9 And if thine eye offend thee, pluck it out, and cast it from thee: it is better for thee to enter into life with one eye, rather than having two eyes to be cast into hell fire.

Jesus said that the fires of Hell would never be quenched.

Mar. 9:43 And if thy hand offend thee, cut it off: it is better for thee to enter into life maimed, than having two hands to go into hell, into the fire that never shall be quenched:

We have learned in Chapter 11 that the fires of Hell will never be quenched because they will be added to the Lake of Fire. They will burn forever just as Jesus said.

Jesus said Hell would be filled with sorrows.

Mat. 13:50 And shall cast them into the furnace of fire: there shall be wailing and gnashing of teeth.

Hell is loud, as the souls suffering there scream in agony. The pain will cause them to clench their teeth but to no avail, the flames will not stop tormenting them.

Jesus said the "worms" in Hell cannot die.

Mar. 9:44 Where their worm dieth not, and the fire is not quenched.

Jesus said Hell had an area with darkness.

Mat. 8:12 But the children of the kingdom shall be cast out into outer darkness: there shall be weeping and gnashing of teeth.

This is the darkness that Christ was in when He suffered in the torment side of Hell.

Psa. 88:6 Thou hast laid me in the lowest pit, in darkness, in the deeps.

Jesus frequently warned Israel about the dangers of being cast into Hell.

Mat. 5:22b but whosoever shall say, Thou fool, shall be in danger of hell fire.

Mar. 9:45 And if thy foot offend thee, cut it off: it is better for thee to enter halt into life, than having two feet to be cast into hell, into the fire that never shall be quenched:

- The use of Hell during the Millennial Kingdom -

Jesus gave instruction about the purpose Hell will have in the millennial kingdom. After the tribulation, Jesus Christ will set up His kingdom in Jerusalem. At this time He will judge His people.

Mat. 13:49-50 So shall it be at the end of the world: the angels shall come forth, and sever the wicked from among the just,
And shall cast them into the furnace of fire: there shall be wailing and gnashing of teeth.

Christ will send His angels to gather the wicked.

Mat. 24:40-41 Then shall two be in the field; the one shall be taken, and the other left.

Two women shall be grinding at the mill; the one shall be taken, and the other left.

The "one" taken in the above verses is the wicked, who will be cast into Hell, the "furnace of fire". The wicked will be cast into Hell where there will be "weeping and gnashing of teeth".

We see this judgment again in the parable of the marriage feast.

Mat. 22:11-13 And when the king came in to see the guests, he saw there a man which had not on a wedding garment:
And he saith unto him, Friend, how camest thou in hither not having a wedding garment? And he was speechless.
Then said the king to the servants, Bind him hand and foot, and take him away, and cast him into outer darkness; there shall be weeping and gnashing of teeth.

Those who are not ready for the King will be taken away and "cast" into "outer darkness".

Mat. 8:11-12 And I say unto you, That many shall come from the east and west, and shall sit down with Abraham, and Isaac, and Jacob, in the kingdom of heaven.
But the children of the kingdom shall be cast out into outer darkness: there shall be weeping and gnashing of teeth.

The men who are not worthy of the kingdom will be cast out. They will not be allowed entry into the kingdom.

136

They will be taken out, away from the light of the kingdom, and into darkness. Thus, Jesus calls it, "outer darkness"; darkness that is found outside of the kingdom. Jesus warned Israel about their impending judgment. He said it would be better to cut off your hand than to let your hand cause you to be cast into Hell.

Mat. 5:29-30 And if thy right eye offend thee, pluck it out, and cast it from thee: for it is profitable for thee that one of thy members should perish, and not that thy whole body should be cast into hell.
And if thy right hand offend thee, cut it off, and cast it from thee: for it is profitable for thee that one of thy members should perish, and not that thy whole body should be cast into hell.

This is a literal amputation, as it would be better for one to enter the kingdom with one hand, than having two and be cast into Hell. It will be better to enter the kingdom maimed, blind, deaf, dumb, or with any other physical problem because they would be healed and made whole in the kingdom as prophesied in Isaiah 35.[50]

Isa. 35:5-6 Then the eyes of the blind shall be opened, and the ears of the deaf shall be unstopped.
Then shall the lame man leap as an hart, and the tongue of the dumb sing: for in the wilderness shall waters break out, and streams in the desert.

- Hell made visible -

---

[50]One of the purposes of the healing ministry of Christ was to prepare Israel for entry into the kingdom. There would not be any blind, deaf, lame, etc... all would be made whole.

During the kingdom, Hell will be a visible reminder of God's perfect justice as evidenced by Isaiah in chapter 66.

Isa. 66: 23-24 And it shall come to pass, that from one new moon to another, and from one sabbath to another, shall all flesh come to worship before me, saith the LORD.
And they shall go forth, and look upon the carcases of the men that have transgressed against me: for their worm shall not die, neither shall their fire be quenched; and they shall be an abhorring unto all flesh.

During the kingdom, "all flesh" is commanded to come before the Lord in Jerusalem to worship Him. This worship is to take place on a regular basis, "from one new moon to another, and from one sabbath to another". They will then "go forth" out of the city and come to a place where they will look upon the "carcases" (worms) that have "transgressed against" the Lord. They will be looking straight into Hell. Jesus, when talking about Hell in Mark 9, uses similar wording when He says, "Where their worm dieth not, and the fire is not quenched". Jesus was talking about Hell in Mark 9 as Isaiah is in chapter 66.

Mar. 9: 43-44 And if thy hand offend thee, cut it off: it is better for thee to enter into life maimed, than having two hands to go into hell, into the fire that never shall be quenched:
Where their worm dieth not, and the fire is not quenched.

They will be able to look down into Hell because God will have provided a shaft of some type that leads straight to the pit that allows for viewing.[51] They will see the "worms" in unquenchable fire and they will be abhorred.[52]

This opening will probably be large, as "all flesh" will be coming to look into Hell and see the "worms". The whole world is commanded to witness the souls suffering in Hell.

The "worms" shall "be an abhorring unto all flesh". The meaning of the word abhor or abhorring is to detest with great hatred, loath, or to have extreme contempt. All flesh looking at the "worms" are to abhor them. God does not instruct all flesh to view them with sorrow, sadness, pity, or sympathy but with abhorrence.

All men should abhor the things God abhors and love the things that God loves. This is what it means to fear the Lord. God abhors those in Hell because they Have "transgressed" against Him and commands "all flesh" to abhor them as He does.

Pro. 8:13 The fear of the LORD is to hate evil: pride, and arrogancy, and the evil way, and the froward mouth, do I hate.

Man should have the same attitude as God does toward those in Hell.

---

[51] This shaft maybe much like the opening of the earth that swallowed Korah and his followers. Num. 16:32.

[52] It is probable, that during the kingdom, the form of execution will be casting the condemned alive into the pit of Hell.

The visible Hell should cause men to fear God during the millennial kingdom.

Did Jesus really mean Hell?

Some have questioned the use of the word Hell by Jesus in the gospels. They point out that Jesus uses a different word in the Greek, "Gehenna", than that used in the Old Testament, "Hades"/"Sheol". Because of this, some believe that Christ was not talking about the actual Hell in the center of the earth; but, about the Lake of Fire. This teaching leads to confusion. It also causes believers to question the truthfulness of their Bible.

Lets look at the word "Gehenna" and we will see why Jesus chose to use that word in describing the Hell in the middle of the earth.

"Gehenna" is commonly known as a valley near Jerusalem, which became the city dump. The garbage of the city was taken here and dumped into this valley and burned. This matches perfectly with the warning Jesus was teaching about Hell during the kingdom. Those who are judged as wicked are to be taken out of the city and dumped into the garbage dump of mankind, Hell. Just as the burning of the garbage was visible to the Jews, so shall the burning of those who are cast into Hell be visible to those who look upon them. This is why Christ used the word "Gehenna". He was talking about the role Hell, the literal Hell in the center of the earth, would have in the kingdom.

In addition, there is not a verse in the scriptures that links "gehenna" with the Lake of Fire; it is always used in relation to Hell in the earth.

If one wants to believe that Christ was referring to the Lake of Fire and not Hell, another problem arises. We have seen how Christ will judge men during the millennial kingdom and cast them out. If Christ was talking about the Lake of Fire, He will be casting these men into the Lake of Fire and not to Hell. But this cannot be. The scriptures tell us that all unrighteous men will be judged at the Great White Throne Judgment. It is after this judgment that men will be cast into the Lake of Fire. No man will be cast into the Lake of Fire before the Great White Throne Judgment. It would be unjust of God to eternally punish men in the Lake of Fire without their day in court. Therefore Christ cannot be casting men into the Lake of Fire during the millennial kingdom; He must be casting them into Hell, just as the Bible states.

Jesus did teach about the Lake of Fire.

Mat. 25:41 Then shall he say also unto them on the left hand, Depart from me, ye cursed, into everlasting fire, prepared for the devil and his angels:

Jesus stated that there is an "everlasting fire" that has been "prepared for the devil and his angels". This is the Lake of Fire. This eternal punishment was designed for Satan and those who followed in his rebellion. **Jesus is teaching that man will now, too, be cast into the Lake of Fire. This is a horrifying revelation from God.**

When Jesus spoke in this passage, He had an eternal viewpoint. We know this because of the following verse.

Mat. 25:46 And these shall go away into everlasting punishment: but the righteous into life eternal.

The men who Christ will cast out will "go into everlasting punishment", while others will have "life eternal". Jesus was teaching about the eternal destiny of all men. Men whom Christ will cast into Hell during the millennial kingdom will eternally find their home in the "everlasting fire", Lake of Fire. This is sobering and should cause all men to fear God and accept His wonderful gift of salvation.

APPENDIX 3

THE BOTTOMLESS PIT

The location of the bottomless pit is in the center of Hell, in the center of the earth. The scriptures tell us more about what is currently in the bottomless pit.

The bottomless pit has a door over it. This door is shut, sealed, and locked. This bottomless pit is not empty but is filled with terrifying locusts.

Rev. 9:2-3 And the fifth angel sounded, and I saw a star fall from heaven unto the earth: and to him was given the key of the bottomless pit.
And he opened the bottomless pit; and there arose a smoke out of the pit, as the smoke of a great furnace; and the sun and the air were darkened by reason of the smoke of the pit.
And there came out of the smoke locusts upon the earth: and unto them was given power, as the scorpions of the earth have power

These locusts are alive and wait in this pit for a day when they will be released. These locusts are described in Revelation.

Rev. 9:7-10 And the shapes of the locusts were like unto horses prepared unto battle; and on their heads were as it were crowns like gold, and their faces were as the faces of men.
And they had hair as the hair of women, and their teeth were as the teeth of lions.

And they had breastplates, as it were breastplates of iron; and the sound of their wings was as the sound of chariots of many horses running to battle.

And they had tails like unto scorpions, and there were stings in their tails: and their power was to hurt men five months.

These locusts are real and will one day be released during the tribulation to torment and hurt mankind for a period of 5 months. They are unlike any locusts upon the earth now. These creatures will seek the flesh of men. They will sting men; their poison will hurt the people they sting. This pain will be real and intense.

Rev. 9:6 And in those days shall men seek death, and shall not find it; and shall desire to die, and death shall flee from them.

It will become so painful that men will seek death to try and escape the pains they are suffering. It is interesting to note that these men do not cry out to God in repentance; but, instead seek death as their way of escape. We see this same attitude of rebellion and unrepentance throughout the book of Revelation as men experience God's judgment.

The Bible speaks of a king over these abominable creatures.

Rev. 9:11 And they had a king over them, which is the angel of the bottomless pit, whose name in the Hebrew tongue is Abaddon, but in the Greek tongue hath his name Apollyon.

These locusts have an angel, Abaddon, who is identified as a king over them. This king, Abaddon, is called the "angel of the bottomless pit". This king is not Satan because Satan is not an angel; he is a cherubim - Eze. 28:14.

Eze. 28:14a Thou art the anointed cherub that covereth; and I have set thee so:

Appendix 4

THE EAST WIND

The scriptures teach of an "east wind" which blows across the face of the earth as a tempest. This "east wind" catches all the unrighteous souls of men and thrusts them down into Hell.

God uses the "east wind" to execute His destructive power. We see the "east wind" being used to blast the corn of the earth for seven years during the time of Joseph.

Gen. 41:23 And, behold, seven ears, withered, thin, and blasted with the east wind, sprung up after them:

Gen. 41:27 And the seven thin and ill favoured kine that came up after them are seven years; and the seven empty ears blasted with the east wind shall be seven years of famine.

The "east wind" also brought the locust that plagued Egypt.

Ex. 10:13 And Moses stretched forth his rod over the land of Egypt, and the LORD brought an east wind upon the land all that day, and all that night; and when it was morning, the east wind brought the locusts.

God used the "east wind" to destroy the ships of Tarshis.

Psa. 48:7 Thou breakest the ships of Tarshish with an east wind.

Isaiah calls the "east wind" the "rough wind".

Isa. 27:8 In measure, when it shooteth forth, thou wilt debate with it: he stayeth his rough wind in the day of the east wind.

The "east wind" is known as "the wind of the Lord".

Hsa. 13:15 Though he be fruitful among his brethren, an east wind shall come, the wind of the LORD shall come up from the wilderness, and his spring shall become dry, and his fountain shall be dried up: he shall spoil the treasure of all pleasant vessels.

When God uses "wind" to destroy or bring evil, He always uses the "east wind", the "wind of the Lord". God uses the "east wind" to catch the souls of unrighteous men because it is His wind, "the wind of the LORD", and none can escape it.

To contact the author please visit the web site:

http://www.grace-harbor-church.org

There you will find material for both children and adults including free Bible studies and downloadable messages from the author.

Another book by Gary Paul Miller

Could all of the religions of the world have originated from just one person?

Was that person Cain? And if so how did he do it?

What really happened between Cain and Abel? And, who does the Lord Jesus Christ say killed Abel?

The founder of all religion will be revealed and the "way" he established exposed.

www.grace-harbor-church.org